VISIONARY SCIENCE

VISIONARY SCIENCE

A Translation of Tillich's
''On the Idea of a Theology of Culture''

with an Interpretive Essay

Tillich, Paul

Victor Nuovo

Wayne State University Press   Detroit   1987

Library of Congress Cataloging-in-Publication Data

Tillich, Paul, 1886–1965.
  Visionary science.

  Includes index.
  1. Christianity and culture.   I. Nuovo, Victor,
1931–   . II. Title.
BR115.C8T4813 1987   261   87-25352
ISBN 0-8143-1940-8 (alk.)

For Betty, the love of my life

Contents

Preface

This book originated spontaneously from a reading of Paul Tillich's programmatic essay, "On the Idea of a Theology of Culture." Having had occasion to compare the current English translation with the German text, I discovered a misreading in the translation that, when put right, brought to light a much more radical motive in Tillich's thinking than I was accustomed to or than one would expect to find from reading standard interpretations of Tillich's thinking—interpretations that, for the most part, reflect an image of his life and work that an older Tillich, with more than a little help from his friends, fashioned for posterity. Rereading the text in the light of this discovery, I was made aware also of Tillich's ambivalence toward his radicalness and the consequences of this divided attitude upon his efforts to develop a new theological program. The results of my attempt to expound these consequences—which I am confident are more than idiosyncratic to Tillich, but are of great moment for theology, philosophical and dogmatic, in this century—are set forth in this book.

I am glad for the opportunity that this preface provides to acknowledge my debt to those who in several important ways have aided me in this work. A grant from the American Philosophical Society supported some initial researches that preceded and laid the foundation for this work; Middlebury College provided released time, a leave of absence, and financial support. Maria Grossmann, formerly librarian of the Andover Harvard Library, gave me ready access to materials in the Tillich Archive and encouragement to pursue my work. Robert C. Kimball, Tillich's literary executor, gave me permission to publish my translation of Tillich's text. My colleague, Lynne Baker, read part of the manuscript and helped me to bring clarity to my argument and to some basic concepts. I am especially grateful to Robert Mandel, the director of Wayne State University Press, whose sustained interest in my work gave me support when it was most needed.

Introduction

The principal aim of this study is to present a critical reading of a
text, one that—in spite of its youthfulness, its uncertain vision,
and manifold flaws—is of the utmost importance to theology in
this century. At issue is the fate of theology. This issue is still
undecided after almost three quarters of a century, and the circumstances that prevailed then, when Tillich first addressed it,
seem hardly to have changed except to become more ominous
and, hence, make the prospect for theology seem much less hope-
ful. Theologians, including Tillich, have not been unproductive
since this text was written. Their achievements, by all standards,
are impressive but their influence has not taken hold, at least in
ways that they might have intended or at least hoped. Whether
because of what they have written or because of the circumstances within which their writings must now be read and understood, their affirmations, which once seemed clear and certain,
have become uncertain and ambiguous, so much so that many of
their most able successors have come to the conclusion that the
only honorable task left to the theologian is to dismantle theology. Not long ago, when I reread this text, I was most impressed
by how much it reflects just this situation. Here Tillich argues
with great cogency that theologians must not presume to discourse about some real object or to be the privileged possessors of
a certain truth immune from the uncertainties of our existence;
that realism and positivism in theology are illusions and that the
theologian first of all has to dispel them for himself and others
and, having done so, being free yet also earthy in a new and
revalued way, he may then find his proper work in envisioning

earth's future, which is the primary work of the theologian of culture.

This, I believe, is the message of Tillich's text and the reason it remains basic not only to his life's work but to theology in this century. But, succinct summaries, however accurate they may be, must not take the place of texts. If a text is important, then it must be read, studied, and appropriated. And, this is what I have tried to do here. Moreover, critical interpretation is called for especially in the case of this text, because however unmistakable its message, it is not presented unambiguously, and this ambiguity, which occurs in inconsistencies of argument and attitude, is as much a part of the text and its significance as what I take to be its still clear message.

Reading Tillich is not easy. Quite apart from the usual difficulties of reading any philosophical or theological text—the level of abstraction, the complexity of the arguments, and the historical background that must be provided to understand basic concepts and issues—there are special difficulties that pertain to Tillich's writing. His texts are invariably compact and notoriously systematic. The latter quality has a force that propels one through the text, overwhelming the questioning and doubting spirit, dispersing perplexity and forcing upon one the illusion of insight and understanding. Tillich is often easy to summarize but difficult to explain. On reflection, what first seemed conceptually clear later appears vague and what seemed logically well formed, a perplexing disorder. These difficulties are compounded by many allusions to other texts and traditions, present and past, many of which Tillich himself may have been only vaguely aware. They add to the conceptual richness of his writing, but also to its confusion.

To present a text of this complexity requires that it be accompanied by an interpretation. In this instance, since I am writing for English-language readers, the text also had to be translated from its original German. Although an English translation has been made and published,[1] I am unable to recommend it or to use it here. The translation that appears here is new, made by me from the text as originally published.[2] In the interpretation that follows the text, I have tried to account for every sentence whose meaning seemed at all unclear to me. However, I have not followed the rather tedious method of a line-by-line interpretation. I have written an interpretative essay, not a commentary. It is meant to be read continuously. Each chapter of the essay corresponds to a numbered section of the text. My hope is that whoever reads my essay will first read Tillich's text, preferably more than once, and will have it in mind as well in hand while reading the interpretation.

In spite of its length, the interpretation is selective in its treatment of Tillich's text. I have focused primarily on its line of argument and conceptual content, keeping before me, as much as possible, Tillich's overall strategy. I have only dealt minimally with the sources and influences that were at work here. To have done otherwise would have required me to digress into lengthy justifications, for on the question of sources, Tillich provides little help to his readers. It is rare that one finds him, in his writings, reading a text. More often than not, his allusions and references are broad and vague, so that one must become the master of a tradition in considerable detail before one can trace Tillich's thoughts back to their historical sources. This is one great reward of reading Tillich. In the effort to understand him, one learns much more. Reading him, one has the sense of being surrounded by a great host of spirits, but often this presence is unsettlingly ghostly, the spirits change identity or disappear when one reaches out to touch them. The reader's knowledge must give substance to these spirits. I am working now on Tillich's intellectual biography; there, I shall attempt to provide what is lacking here in sources and influences.

However, not to leave the question of Tillich's sources altogether to the future, I offer the following brief account. Philosophically, Tillich is an idealist, which is to say, for him, consciousness and its objects and even the ground of consciousness, which is its ultimate object, are spiritual; that is, free, creative, self-positing being. And there is only one spirit, which in its self-development becomes many before returning to its actualized self. For Tillich, the ground of consciousness (substance, metaphysical content, the absolute of meaning), which is his ruling Idea and is the Truth of everything or at least of every experience, always comes to expression in a thinking thing, an individual consciousness that seems to itself self-contained and yet lacks self-certainty. This conscious individual is divided against itself, fragmented, and estranged from its ultimate ground. Consciousness becomes reconciled with its ground not by its own means but by a power that is like grace, that proceeds not from beyond and without but from deep within. This gracious reconciling power is transcendent, although not supernaturally transcendent. For idealists, and hence, for Tillich, transcendence is always self-transcendence. Finally, as the ultimate metaphysical principle, it is not separate from nature or from human nature, but, in a manner that recalls Spinoza, is nature's ground, a productive power that redeems as it creates and works always from inner to outer. Thus, it would appear that Tillich is neither, strictly speaking, Fichtean (although there are traces of Fichte's thought in his idea of creation as a self-positing act, and perhaps Tillich's Fichteanism makes him receptive to Nietzsche) nor Hegelian (although Tillich's attempt to establish a standpoint for science is vaguely Hegelian, and his understanding of Expressionist painting is reminiscent of Hegel's characterization of Romantic art, which, given the importance of Expressionism in Tillich's own intellectual development, is not an insignificant observation). Tillich's thought seems much closer to the later Schelling (see Chapter 4 of the Interpretation); although it is more explicitly Augustinian and Lutheran in its anthropology, less speculative, and more Kantian in its moral emphasis. Finally, Tillich's thought must be counted preeminently among efforts in this century to develop a theological modernism and, therefore, is receptive to all the influences that contributed to modernism. In this connection, we must not fail to include in this rich mixture of Tillich's sources, Nietzsche's tragicomic heroic picture of the seer and creator Zarathustra, the advocate of earth, along with Nietzschean ideas of historical relativism, perspectivism, and ecstatic fatalism. We also must include the philosophy of life as developed by Dilthey and neo-Kantian theories of culture, especially those of Windelband and Rickert and Simmel. To demonstrate specifically which of these sources and traditions entered his thinking, and in what combinations and under what circumstances, would require a much longer work than this, with many inconclusive arguments and digressions on each point of plausible influence. Even in those rare moments where Tillich cites a specific text, we cannot be sure that he is thinking with it or even against it (as Heidegger characteristically does); more often than not, the text seems incidental to his thinking, its contents having been assimilated and made, above all, Tillichean.

I also have chosen not to dwell on the question of sources because I did not want to risk losing sight of the principal aim of my essay. In this study, translation and interpretation are subservient to appropriation. To appropriate something is to make it one's own, to give it a living presence. Emerson understood this well.[3] Ownership of a text, of any cultural creation, is not an exclusive right. Someone writes it and lets it go. Others take it and read it and make it their own. The right way to appropriate a text is to give it a presence that can be shared in equally and creatively by everyone. It is only when texts and other cultural objects are made into commodities to be bought and sold that they become someone's exclusive property. But, then, this is also to defile them. Appropriation requires something more than careful analysis; it calls for a rekindling of its spirit through a rediscovery of its intentions. This I have tried to do. Whether successfully or not, others no doubt will decide.

To read a text as closely as I have this one often leads to violence. Interpretation and appropriation often are violent acts. They dismember and consume. These fashionable metaphors may be shocking, but they also are honest. It is a necessary violence, if the past is to be brought to life in the present; if appropriation of the past is not to be a slavish, unthinking, disrespectful, and merely imitative replay of once inspired thoughts; if historical existence is to be enriched by the past and yet remain free. Surely this violence is not comparable to poisoning philosophers or burning heretics or subjecting dissenters to torture—nor is it exclusive of deep respect and genuine praise. A meaner kind of violence is caused by the frustration of struggling with a text that will not give up its meaning easily, and this frustration becomes intense in those moments of discovery, when it turns out that the confusion is not in oneself but in the text. Then, one desires revenge, demands retribution, gloats over one's small victory, attaches one's victim to the chariot of one's thought and drags him about the field of battle. I will not deny that I have been guilty of such dishonor, and I cannot excuse myself by claiming to play Achilles to Tillich's Hector. As Heidegger somewhere observed, it is more often common minds that gloat when they have won small victories over great minds, but even the greatest thinkers make mistakes and it would be as much a dishonor to them to ignore these mistakes, or worse, to gloss over them. There are mistakes in Tillich's thinking as presented in this text. Some of them are not insignificant. I have not looked away from them. They have caused me frustration, even anger. I hope that I will not be found gloating too often. For my intention is to praise Tillich, not by adding epithets to his name or by being party to the formation of a sterile Tillichean orthodoxy, but by taking his thought seriously. Appropriation is praise.

NOTES

1. "On the Idea of a Theology of Culture." English translation by William Baillie Green, in Paul Tillich, *What is Religion?*, edited by James Luther Adams (New York, 1969).

2. "Ueber die idee einer Theologie der Kultur" in Gustav Radbruch and Paul Tillich, *Religionsphilosophie der Kultur* (Berlin, 1919). The publication is number 24 of the *Philosophische Vortraege* of the Kant-Gesellschaft. Tillich's contribution to this publication was the text of an address given on April 16, 1919. The text has been reprinted with slight modifications in Tillich's *Gesammelte Werke*, Vol. IX.

3. Cf., Emerson's "History," in Ralph Waldo Emerson, *Essays and Lectures*, edited by Joel Porte (New York, 1983).

On the Idea of a Theology of Culture
Paul Tillich

Ladies and Gentlemen!

1. THEOLOGY AND PHILOSOPHY OF RELIGION

Among the experiential sciences, standpoints are things that must be overcome. Actuality is the criterion of truth, and actuality is one. Of two contradictory standpoints, only one can be true or both false. The progress of scientific experience decides. It has decided that the earth is a body suspended in space and not a floating plate, that the five books of Moses originated from various sources not from Moses. Standpoints that have opposed these conclusions are in error. It has not yet been decided who is the author of the letter to the Hebrews. Of the different suppositions, one or none is true.

It is otherwise among the systematic cultural sciences. *Among them, the standpoint of the systematic thinker belongs to the thing itself;* it is a moment in the history of the development of culture; it is a definite concrete historical realization of a cultural idea; it is not only cognizant of culture but also creative of it. Here the alternation "true or false" loses its validity, for the attitudes of spirit to actuality are manifold: there is a gothic and a baroque aesthetics, a catholic and a modern protestant dogmatics; a romantic and a puritan ethics can never be designated simply true or false. For this reason, it is also impossible to form universal concepts of cultural ideas. What religion or art may be cannot be experienced by means of abstraction: abstraction nullifies what is essential, namely, the concrete forms, and necessarily disregards every concretion that is still to come. *Every cultural-scientific universal concept is either unusable or it is a concealed normative concept;* it is either a paraphrase of nothing or it is the expression of a standpoint; it is either a worthless shell or it is a creation.—A stand-point is expressed by an individual; but if it involves more than individual choice, if it is creation, then it is also—in a greater or lesser degree—creation by a circle in which the individual stands; and since this circle with its own intellectuality or spirituality is not without spiritual circles that surround it, and creations of the past on which it depends, the most individual standpoint is firmly planted in the soil of the objective spirit that is the mother soil of every cultural creation. From this soil, the concrete standpoint derives the universal forms of spiritual reality, while, at the same time, it discovers its own concrete-objective boundaries drawn by circles that—observed from there—seem ever more narrowly to circumscribe it and by the historical endowments of concrete spirituality, until in a creative self-positing act, it fashions a new, individual, and unique synthesis of universal form and concrete content. Corresponding to this process are three forms of nonem-pirical cultural science: philosophy of culture, which attends to the universal forms, the a priori of all culture; philosophy of the history of cultural values, which forms the transition from the universal forms to its own individual standpoint, which it thereby justifies; and finally normative-cultural science, which brings the concrete standpoint to a systematic expression.

Thus, we must distinguish between philosophy of art, that is, a phenomenological, critical-philosophical presentation of the essence or value that the term 'Art' denotes, on the one hand, and, on the other, aesthetics, that is, a systematic-normative pre-sentation of the things that must be counted as beautiful. Or, we must distinguish between moral philosophy, which asks What is morality? and normative ethics, which asks What is moral? And, likewise, between philosophy of religion and theology. *Theology, therefore, is the concrete normative science of religion.* This is the sense in which the concept is meant in this context, and, in my opinion, only in this sense can a claim be made for its scientific utility. This implies a twofold denial. First, theology is not a science with a special object singled out from among others, and which we call god. The critique of reason has put an end to such a science. It also has brought theology down from heaven to earth. Theology is a part of the science of religion, namely, the systematic-normative part.—Second, theology is not the presentation of a particular complex of revelation. This conception presupposes a supernatural-authoritative concept of revelation that has been overcome by a wave of religious-historical insights and by the logical and religious critique of abstract supernaturalism.

Accordingly, the task of theology is to project a normative system of religion from the perspective of a concrete standpoint, by building upon the ground of the categories of the philosophy of religion and embedding the individual standpoint within the confessional, universal religious-historical, and intellectual historical circles. This is not concealed rationalism, for it acknowledges the concrete-religious standpoint, and it is not concealed supernaturalism, as is still the case with our critical-historical school, for it is the philosophical-historical breakthrough of every authoritative limitation of the individual standpoint. It is oriented towards Nietzsche's conception of the "creative" on the soil of Hegel's "objective-historical spirit."

One more remark about the relation of the philosophy of culture and the normative systematics of culture: They belong together and stand in correlation. Not only is theology oriented towards the philosophy of religion, but the converse is also the case. As I said in the beginning, every universal philosophical concept, which is not conceived as a normative concept on a concrete basis, is empty. The distinction between philosophy and a science of norms does not lie in this; rather, they differ in the direction in which they work. Philosophy works out universal, a priori, and categorical concepts on the broadest empirical basis and in systematic relation with other values and concepts of essence. The normative sciences work up the special content and the principles that determine value into special systems for every cultural science.

From the power of a concrete, creative realization, the highest universal concept gains its rich and yet encompassing vitality, and from the comprehensive fullness of a highest universal concept, the normative system derives its objective scientific significance: set in every universal concept there is a normative concept, and set in every creative normative concept there is a universal concept. This is the dialectic of the systematic science of culture.

2. CULTURE AND RELIGION

In the past, systematic theology comprised theological ethics as well as dogmatics. In modern theology, the system usually divides into apologetics, dogmatics, and ethics. What kind of a science is this curiosity that takes its place alongside philosophical ethics and calls itself theological? One can give different answers to this question. One can say that philosophical ethics is concerned with the essence of morality, not with moral norms, and then draw the distinction between the two as one between moral philosophy and normative ethics. But why should normative ethics be theological? Philosophy, or, better, the science of culture, cannot let the task of writing its own normative ethics be taken away from it. If both should now appear valid, we would have admitted the old doctrine of twofold truth into the sphere of ethics as a basic principle.—But, there is another answer: the moral life also wants to become concrete. In ethics, too, there must be a standpoint that is not only the standpoint of an individual, but which rather originates from a concrete ethical community together with its historical contexts. Such a community is the church.

This answer is correct wherever the church is the dominant cultural community, wherever there is a church-directed culture and where not only ethics, but also science, art, and social life is led, censored, restricted, and systematized by the church. But, in protestant countries, the church long ago abandoned any claim to this role. It acknowledges that there is a dominant cultural community outside the church, in which the individual standpoint is rooted in the general standpoint of the cultural community. There is just as little place for a system of ethics based upon theological principles as there is for German, or Aryan, or bourgeois ethics, aesthetics, science, or sociology, even though these concretions naturally play an important role in the factical shaping of the individual standpoint. Once the church has recognized in principle a secular culture, there can little more be a theological ethics than there can be a theological logic or aesthetics or sociology.

My claim is this: *what until recently was the intention of theological ethics can only find fulfillment in a theology of culture, which is related not only to ethics but to every cultural function. Not theological ethics, but theology of culture.* This, at the outset, calls for a few remarks on the relation of culture and religion. Religion has the peculiar property of not belonging to any particular psychic function; neither the Hegelian conception of religion, which assigns it to the theoretical faculty, nor the Kantian conception, which assigns it to the practical faculty, nor the Schleiermacherian conception, which assigns it to feeling, have been able to be maintained. The last comes closest to the truth, because it expresses the indifference of what is authentically religious towards its cultural expressions. But, feeling accompanies every cultural experience, and one does not for that reason call it religious. If, however, a specific feeling is meant, then along with its determination a theoretical or practical moment has already been given. Religion is not a feeling, rather it is an activity of spirit in which something practical, something theoretical, and something emotional are joined together into a complex unity. If, now, we divide the cultural functions—and in my opinion this is the most nearly correct systematization—into one kind of function by which spirit receives the object into itself, namely, the intellectual and aesthetic functions conceived together as theoretical in the sense of theoria, that is, intuition, and another kind by which spirit tries to enter the object in order to shape it to suit itself, namely the individual and social ethical functions (including law and society), hence, the practical functions, it follows that religion can only find its actuality in relation to a theoretical or to a practical activity. *The religious potency, that is, a certain quality of consciousness, must be distinguished from the religious act, that is, from an autonomous theoretical or practical event that has this quality.* By uniting religious principle and cultural function, a specifically religious sphere can now arise, religious knowledge: myth or dogma; a realm of religious aesthetics: cultus; religious formation of the person: sanctification; a religious form of society: the church together with the ecclesiastical law and the ethics of community peculiar to it. In such forms, religion is actual; only in unity with extra-religious cultural functions does the religious principle have existence. The religious principle is not one principle among others in the life of spirit. The absolute character of

every religious consciousness would break through such limitations. *But religion is actual in every spiritual domain.* However, from
what has been said, a new limitation seems to be given. In every
province of the life of spirit, there is now given a special circle, a
special sphere of religious influence. How are these spheres to be
delimited? Here, in fact, lie the great cultural conflicts between
church and state, between religious community and society, art
and cultus, science and dogma, which have filled the early centuries of the modern era and even now have not completely come
to an end. A conflict is not possible as long as the cultural functions are kept under the sway of a religious heteronomy. It is
overcome as soon as the cultural functions have struggled successfully for their autonomy. Where, then, does this leave religion? The autonomy of the life of spirit is threatened, indeed it is
annulled, as long as there is dogma, in whatever form, alongside
science, "community" alongside society, church alongside state,
all claiming separate spheres for themselves. For this gives rise to
a twofold truth as well as to a twofold morality and a twofold
justice, one of which, in each case, is born not from the principles
of legitimacy of each cultural function but from an alien religious
law. This doubleness must under all circumstances be annulled.
As soon as it enters consciousness it becomes intolerable, for it
destroys consciousness.

The solution of this problem can be derived only from the
concept of religion. I will try to present the concept of religion
that is presupposed here but without justifying it—for to do so
would require a short course in the philosophy of religion. Religion is the experience of the unconditioned, and this means the
experience of absolute reality founded on the experience of absolute nothingness. One experiences the nothingness of entities, the
nothingness of values, the nothingness of the personal life. Wherever this experience has brought one to the nothingness of an
absolute radical No, there it is transformed into an experience, no
less absolute, of reality, into a radical Yes. This Yes has nothing to
do with a new reality that stands beside or above things; such a
reality would only be a thing of a higher order, which in its turn
would become subject to the power of the No. Rather, throughout everything, the reality forces itself upon us that is simul-

taneously a No and a Yes to things. It is not a being, it is not substance, it is not the totality of beings. It is, to use a mystical formulation, what is beyond being, what is simultaneously and absolutely nothing and something. *Nevertheless, even the predicate 'is' conceals what is at issue here, because it is not a question of some actual being that concerns us, but of an actuality of meaning, indeed, the ultimate and most profound actuality of meaning that convulses everything and builds everything anew.*

From this point of view, it becomes immediately clear that one cannot speak properly of a special religious sphere of culture. If it is the essence of this religious basic experience to deny the whole sphere of knowledge and all the while to affirm it, then there is no longer any place for knowing in some special religious sense, for some special religious object, for a special religious epistemology. The conflict between dogma and science is overcome. The autonomy of science is preserved entire, religious heteronomy in any shape or form is made impossible. Instead, the whole of science is put under the "theonomy" of the religious basic experience.—It is the same for ethics. It is no longer possible to maintain a personal or communal ethics in a special relation to some religious object alongside individual or social ethics. Ethics, too, is absolutely autonomous, completely free of religious heteronomy and yet altogether "theonomous" in the sense of the religious basic experience. The possibilities of conflict have been radically removed.—The relation of religion and culture, therefore, has been made clear in principle. The special spheres of religious culture have been fundamentally annulled. Whatever significance may yet belong to them is a question whose answer must await the answer to the prior question of the meaning of a theology of culture.

3. THEOLOGY OF CULTURE

In the last discussion, repeated mention had been made of autonomy and theonomy of cultural values. We must inquire further into these concepts; and I also should like to propose that the autonomy of the cultural functions is established in their form, in the laws that govern their employment; theonomy, on the other hand, is established in their substance, the reality that is represented or conveyed by means of these laws. It is now possible to state the law: *the more form, the more autonomy; the more substance, the more theonomy.* However, there cannot be one without the other. A form that forms nothing is just as inconceivable as a substance that is not situated in a form. Any attempt to comprehend substance apart from form would be a reversion to the worst kind of heteronomy. A new form would immediately take shape, and it would enter into opposition to them and limit them in their autonomy. The relation of substance and form must be thought of as a line, one end of which represents pure form, and the other, pure substance. On the line itself, however, they are united. *The revelation of an overwhelming substance occurs in this way: form becomes more and more inadequate for the reality that is supposed to be contained by it, so that this reality in overwhelming abundance shatters it. And yet this overwhelming and this shattering are themselves still form.*

The task of a theology of culture, then, is to trace this process in every sphere and creation of culture and to bring it to expression. But this is to be undertaken not from the standpoint of form, for this would be the task of the appropriate cultural science, rather from the standpoint of substance, as theology of culture and not as cultural systematics. The point is that concrete religious experiences, which are embedded in every great cultural manifestation, be brought to expression and given prominence. Hence, it follows that besides theology, as the normative science of religion, a theological method is required, just as besides systematic psychology there is a psychological method and likewise a sociological method, and so forth. These methods are universally applicable, they are suitable to any object, and yet they have a home, a particular science, into which they are born. *It is the same with the theological method, which is the universal application of theological inquiry into every cultural value.*

Previously, we assigned to theology the task of bringing to systematic expression a concrete religious standpoint, founding it upon the formation of general philosophical-religious concepts and presenting it through the medium of a philosophical-historical classification of religious phenomena. The task of a theology of culture corresponds to this. It carries out a general religious analysis of all cultural creations, it offers a philosophical-historical and typological classification of great cultural creations from the point of view of the religious substance realized in them, and from its own religious standpoint it fashions the ideal design for a culture religiously fulfilled. Therefore, a threefold task devolves upon it corresponding in general to the threefold task of the systematic-cultural sciences and in particular to the systematic science of religion: *(1) A general religious analysis of culture, (2) A religious typology and philosophy of the history of culture, (3) A concrete religious systematization of culture.*

A cultural-theological analysis must consider two things, the first of which is the relation of form and substance. Substance is something other than content. By content, we understand objectivity in its simple essence, which is raised by form into the spiritual-cultural sphere. By substance, however, is to be understood the meaning, the spiritual substantiality, from which alone form receives its significance. Therefore, it can be said that *substance is caught up into content by means of form and brought to expression.* Content is accidental, substance is essential, form mediates. Form must fit its content. Therefore, it is unlikely that the cultivation of form and the cultivation of content would ever be in opposition, rather, they stand together at one pole, but at the other pole stands the cultivation of substance. The shattering of form by substance is identical to content's loss of substantiality, to its becoming something nonessential. Form loses its necessary relation to content, because content disappears before the overwhelming fullness of substance. Hence, form gains a kind of detachment, as though it were free floating, it stands in an immediate relation to substance. It loses its natural and necessary connection to content; by letting itself in its naturalness be shattered by substance, it becomes form in a paradoxical sense. This is the first consideration, for religious reality, with its Yes and No, first comes to light precisely in substance. And this, then, is the second consideration: the relation of the No and the Yes, the connection and the power in which each comes to expression. Here there are infi-

nitely many possibilities, because the connections and the correlations are infinitely rich.

But, there is still further a definite limitation, and this leads
to the second task of the theology of culture, the typological and
philosophical-historical. This limitation is provided by the image
of the line, mentioned earlier, with its formal and substantial
poles. This image leads to three decisive points, from which three
basic types are derived: the two poles and the midpoint in which
form and substance stand in equilibrium. From this, the typology
derives its basic arrangement: *a typically profane and formal cultural
creation, a typically religious-cultural creation in which substance predominates, and a typically classical cultural creation characterized by
equilibrium and harmony.* This general typology leaves room for
intermediate and transitional stages, and it is unusually diverse
because of the variety of forms of concrete religion that enter into
it. If this theory of types is related to the present and put in
systematic relation to the past, there results a philosophical-historical classification, which then leads immediately to the third,
properly speaking systematic task of the theology of culture.

To what extent can the theologian of culture be a religious
systematizer of culture? The question must first be answered from
its negative side. He cannot be a systematizer from the side of the
form of the cultural functions. This would be an unlawful and
heteronomous encroachment upon culture. He can be such only
from the side of substance. But substance attains to cultural deter-
minateness only in form. So far, it must be said that *the theologian
of culture is not directly culturally creative.* Neither in the sphere of
science, nor of morality, nor of jurisprudence, nor of art is he
productive as such. Rather, he takes towards autonomous production a critical, denying, and affirming position on the basis of
his concrete theological standpoint. *With the material at hand, he
sketches out a religious system of culture, separating and joining as
directed by his theological principle.* He also can look beyond the
material at hand, but only in demand, not in fulfillment. He may
reproach the culture at hand, charging that he finds nothing
among its creation that he might acknowledge as an expression of
the substance dwelling within it. He may point generally in the
direction in which he perceives the fulfillment of a genuine re-

ligious culture, but he cannot himself create the system. If he attempts it, then he will thereby cease to be a theologian of culture, and, taking one or more positions, he will become a creator of culture; but, as a consequence, he will enter the rich and entirely autonomous criticism of cultural forms that, repeatedly, by means of its sovereign power, will direct him towards goals entirely different from ones he wanted to reach. Herein lies the demarcation of the systematic task of the theologian of culture. But, precisely from this, he receives his universal significance. Far from every restriction to a determinate sphere, from the standpoint of substance, he is able to bring to expression the comprehensive unity of the cultural functions and to show the connections, which lead from one manifestation of culture to another, through the underlying unity of the substance that is brought to expression in them. *By this means, he can help to realize the unity of culture from the standpoint of substance, just as the philosopher does from the standpoint of pure forms, of the categories.*

Cultural-theological tasks have often been posed and solved by theological, philosophical, literary, and political-cultural analysts (e.g., Simmel); but the task as such has not been comprehended nor its systematic significance recognized. No one has seen that what is at issue here is a cultural synthesis of the highest significance, a synthesis that not only gathers together the different cultural functions, but that also overcomes the culturally destructive contradiction of religion and culture by means of a sketch of a system of religious culture, in which a science that is in itself religious takes the place of the opposition of science and dogma, in which art that is in itself religious takes the place of the separation of art and cultic form, in which a form of the state that is in itself religious takes the place of the dualism of state and church, and so forth. The task of the theology of culture can be comprehended only in the light of this breadth of purpose. Some examples should clarify and develop this theme.

4. CULTURAL-THEOLOGICAL ANALYSES

In what follows, I should like to restrict myself specifically to the first cultural-theological task with occasional incursions into

the second typological part, because I should like to avoid introducing here without justification a concrete theological principle.
This, however, would be necessary if the historical-philosophical
and systematic task of the theology of culture were to be brought
to completion. Nevertheless, some systematic traces will shine
through the analyses.

I begin with a cultural-theological treatment of art, in particular, the expressionist trend in painting, because Expressionism
seems to me to be an especially impressive example of the relation of form and substance discussed earlier, and because the
definitions of those concepts bear the impress of its character.

What is obvious in the first place is that here content has
become altogether meaningless, that is, content in the sense of
the external factuality of things and events. Nature has been
stripped of her appearance. One looks to the ground of nature.
But, says Schelling, dread dwells at the ground of all living things,
and this dread sweeps over us from the pictures of the Ex-
pressionists, who want to do more than merely to annihilate form
for the sake of flowing formless life, as Simmel supposes, *among
whom, rather, a form-destroying religious substance strives after form,
and this to most everyone must seem an incomprehensible and perplexing paradox.* This dread seems to me also to be deepened by a
feeling of guilt, which is to be interpreted not in a strictly ethical
sense, but in a cosmic sense, the guilt of mere existence. Redemption, however, is the passage from particular existence into the
other, the wiping away of individual prominence, the love mysticism of becoming one with all living things.

Thus, in this art, a more profound No and Yes find expression. However, it seems to me that the form-annihilating No
has the upper hand entirely, even though this is not the intention
of the artists, who were stirred by a will to bring forth a new and
unconditional Yes.

That a strong religious passion is striving here after expression can be substantiated by numerous statements of these
artists, and it is no accident when, in the lively debates that these
paintings provoke, the enthusiastic supporters of Expressionism
appeal constantly to world view and religion, indeed, to the bible

itself. The religious meaning of this art is consciously affirmed by and large by its representatives.

Here is an example from science. The autonomous forms of science have been brought to perfect clarity in the neo-Kantian school. Here is a genuinely scientific and—unreligious philosophy. Form rules absolutely. Current thinking wants to get beyond this, but in no sphere of intellectual activity is this more difficult to achieve than here. During the idealistic period, substance, that is, the experience of reality, had too mercilessly overflowed form and not only this, but it fashioned for itself a new form, which, in the name of intuition, opposed the autonomous forms of science. This conflict was not one within science itself, rather it was the ancient one between two modes of cognition: one belonging to a particular religious tradition, the other, secular. It was an instance of heteronomy against which science had to react and, justly, did react in full force. If, just now, wherever the conflict against the materialistic shadow of Idealism has been completely won, a new trend towards intuition is asserting itself, then is the mistrust of science, although understandable, not necessary. For a new intuitive method can never be expected to compete with the autonomous methods of science. It can only enter in where substance itself bursts the form of these methods and opens the way into the metaphysical. *Indeed, metaphysics is nothing other than the paradoxical attempt to put into forms that which surpasses every form, the experience of the unconditioned.* And if we, from here, look back to Hegel—in the present age there is still no great metaphysics—we shall find in him one of the most profound conceptions of the unity of the No and the Yes, to be sure one characterized by the strongly optimistic supremacy of the Yes. Hegel's thought lacks the experience of dread, which deeply pervades Schelling and Schopenhauer and which no modern metaphysics can be without.

We come now to the sphere of practical values, first, to individual ethics. For a theology of culture, Nietzsche should be able to provide a brilliant and characteristic example in this sphere. His apparently absolutely antireligious orientation makes a theological analysis of his doctrine of the formation of the per-

sonality especially interesting. It should now be certain that his
message contains the opposition between an ethics of virtue and
an ethics of grace, and that ever since Jesus' struggle against the
pharisees and Luther's against Rome, there has hardly been a
more violent shattering of ethical forms by substance. "What is
the greatest thing that you can experience? . . . the hour, when
you say: 'What does my virtue matter?' It has not yet caused me
to rage." The virtue, however, that causes one to rage is beyond
virtue and sin. The theological judgment of nothingness stands
mightily over every individual. "You must will to be consumed in
your own flame. How do you expect to become new, if you have
not first become ashes?" But immediately the Yes is heard with
unprecedented fervor, whether as preaching the Overman or as a
hymn to the wedding ring of rings, the ring of eternal recurrence.
This experience of reality, which Nietzsche contrasts with the
personal, transcends individual ethical forms so far that he himself could be called the antimoralist par excellence just as Luther
was branded the greatest of libertines by all whose personal
thinking is confined to the categories of virtue and reward.

From the standpoint of form it is absolutely paradoxical that
an overwhelming metaphysical substance should deprive ethical
contents of their relevance, should shatter their appropriate
forms, and yet from itself offer in these broken forms a higher
mode of becoming a person than could have occurred in these
forms. *The person, who in Nietzsche's sense stands beyond good and
evil, is absolutely considered ''better'' precisely when, relatively and
ethically-formally considered, he is ''worse'' than the ''good and righteous''. This person is ''pious'' whereas the righteous one is
''impious.''*

*In the realm of social ethics, there is everywhere a resurgence of
love mysticism that signifies a theonomous overcoming of autonomous
ethical form,* without a reversion to a specific religious community
of love. Whether in the speeches of idealistic socialists and communists, or in the poems of a Rilke or Werfel, or in Tolstoy's new
preaching of the Sermon on the Mount, everywhere Kantian
formal ethics of reason and humanity has been broken through.
Kant's formulations of ethical autonomy, his demand that one
must do good for the sake of the good, and his formal law of

universal validity are inviolable foundations of autonomous ethics, and no conception of ethics as divine commandment or as the
love that overcomes the law may shake this foundation. But the
content of love overflows the narrow cup of this form in a nev-
erending stream. The world that merely exists as the sum of particulars is negated, it is experienced as an empty shell lacking
reality. Whoever thinks from the standpoint of the individual can
never reach love, for love transcends the individual. Whoever
thinks in terms of purpose does not know what love is, for love is
the experience of pure being, of pure reality. Whoever wants to
set limits to love or impose conditions upon it does not know that
love is universal, cosmic, just because it affirms and comprehends
everything real as real.

And now, the theology of the state: it shows the substance
that is embedded in different forms of the state; it shows how this
substance overgrows the form of the state, or, conversely, how
the form of the state chokes the substance. Rational political theories, from which, in the struggle against theocracy, the autonomous state arose, led to the abstract state hovering above society.
In *Thus Spake Zarathustra,* this modern state is called "the coldest
of all cold monsters." "Faith and love create a people, but the
sword and a hundred appetites create the state"—this is a brilliant characterization of the nonreligious power or utility state.
And, there is no improvement if this abstract, autonomous state is
clothed with all the cultural functions, as Hegel does, and becomes a god on earth, for then spirit itself is made into a thing of
power or utility.—This is the deepest meaning of idealistic "Anarchism": religious substance bursts open the autonomous form
of the state, not in behalf of a new theocracy, but in behalf of a
new theonomy, of a structure that arises from communities and
their spiritual substance. Even this structure is a form of society,
still a state, but it is such through negation, through the shattering
of the autonomous form of the state, and this very paradox is the
form of "Anarchism." Now such a "state," so called in this paradoxical sense, that is erected from the cultural communities, is
the same as what, in a cultural-theological sense is to be designated "church": *the universal human community, which is erected
from the spiritual communities and which bears within itself all of the*

cultural functions and their religious substance, whose teachers are the great creative philosophers, whose priests are artists, whose prophets are visionaries of a new ethics of the person and community, whose bishops are those who lead the community to new goals, whose deacons and almoners are those who guide and create anew economic processes. For even the economy can shatter its pure autonomy and its own purposiveness by means the substance of religious love mysticism, which does not produce for the sake of production but for the sake of mankind, and yet does not heteronomously curtail the process of production, but guides it theonomously as the universal form of what used to be ecclesiastical almsgiving, which together with the concept of the poor has been annulled on the soil of socialism.

With this we shall conclude the series of examples; they have almost grown into an outline of a system of the theology of culture. In any case, they are able to show what is intended.—At this point, one might ask why this whole enterprise is restricted to the analysis of culture, why nature (or technology) is excluded? The answer is that nature, so far as we know, generally can become an object for us only through culture. For us, nature is meaningful only by means of the spiritual functions, and it is as the sum of these functions that we conceive of culture in a subjective as well as an objective sense. Nature's "in itself" is absolutely beyond our reach, and we can never take hold of it so far as to be able to say anything positive about such an "in itself". But, if nature gains reality for us only through culture, then it is possible to speak exclusively of "cultural theology" and to reject a concept like "natural theology." *Whatever in nature is available to religious substance lies within the domain of the cultural functions insofar as they are related to nature:* the religious substance of a "landscape" is a religio-aesthetic phenomenon, the religious substance of a law of astronomy is a religio-scientific phenomenon. Technology can have a religious effect only by means of aesthetic, social-ethical, and legal concepts; but, always what is at issue is a matter of cultural theology. This theology, without further assistance, comprehends the whole of nature and technology. A natural theology, strictly speaking, would presuppose the mythology of "nature in itself," which is to say, it is unthinkable.

5. THEOLOGY OF CULTURE AND THEOLOGY OF THE CHURCH

One question, which has been repeatedly put off, still requires an answer. What is to become of specifically religious culture, of dogma, cultus, sanctification, community, church? To what extent does there remain a special sphere of the sacred? The answer must proceed from the polar relation between the secular and religious moments of the culture line. In reality, they are never apart, but they are in abstracto distinct, and this distinction is a universal psychological necessity. We are again and again compelled to separate things for our consciousness that are really intertwined so that we might experience something in general about them. We are able to experience religious values in culture, to develop a theology of culture, to distinguish and name the elements of religion, only if a specifically religious culture has preceded us. We can conceive the state as church or art as cultus or science as the doctrine of faith only on the precedent of church, cultus, and dogma. But, something more than precedent is required. We can experience the sacred as somehow distinct from the secular only if we lift it out and set it in a special sphere of cognition, prayer, love, and organization. The secular pole of culture, exact science, formal aesthetics, formal ethics, pure politics, and economics, claims our whole attention unless the opposite pole acts as a counterweight. A universal secularization and profanization of life would be unavoidable unless a sphere of the sacred were constituted in opposition and contradiction to it. This contradiction cannot be overcome so long as form and content must be kept distinct, so long as we are compelled to live in the sphere of reflection and not of intuition. This is one of the most profound and tragic contradictions of cultural life. But, what is great about the development of the last few centuries is that it has taught us to see through it, to deprive it of any real fundamental meaning. Therefore, the contradiction has lost its ultimate severity.

The relation between the theology of culture and church theology follows also from this. Overall, in the development of our topic, we have taken culture as our starting point and have shown how, through the influx of substance into form, culture receives in and for itself a religious quality, and how, finally, in order to preserve and enhance its religious quality, it produces from itself a specific religious sphere of culture, a sphere with a teleological rather than an independently logical dignity. Now for the church theologian, this sphere is given as the expression of a definite religious concreteness. For him, it is not at present something created out of culture, but it has its own independent history. It has developed its own forms, each of which has its own history and independence and continuity in spite of all of the influences of autonomous cultural forms. This is altogether appropriate, but it does not yet decide about the attitude of church theology towards the theology of culture.

There are three possible attitudes that the church theologian can take towards culture. He can subsume it under the concept of "world" and oppose it to the "kingdom of god," which is realized within the church. The result of this is that the specifically religious functions of culture, insofar as they are exercised by the church, partake of the absoluteness of the religious principle, and there is an absolute science, form of art, morality, etc., namely, those realized within the church, in its dogma, its cultus, etc. From the viewpoint of this typically catholic attitude, there can be no way to a theology of culture.

The second attitude is the old protestant one, in which church, cultus, and ethics are set free, their relativity recognized, but the cognitive obligation, absolute science as supernatural revelation, remains binding. However, this attitude has been shaken deeply ever since the theology of the Enlightenment, for it is in principle inconsistent; the preference accorded to the intellectual sphere can no longer be maintained once the absoluteness of its only possible supporter, the church, has been overturned.

The task of present and future protestant theology is to discover the third attitude. This will involve, on the one hand, working out a precise distinction between religious potentiality and actuality, between religious principle and religious culture, and assigning the character of absoluteness only to the religious principle and to no moment of religious culture, not even to one that is historically foundational. On the other hand, present and future protestant theology will conceive its religious principle not only abstractly, leaving its concrete realization to any and every mode of cultural development, rather it will seek to maintain the continuity of its concrete religious standpoint. Only where this attitude is presupposed is there a positive relation between cultural theology and church theology.

In this relation, the church theologian is more conservative, selective, not only forward but also backward looking. "The Reformation continues" is his basic principle, but it is reformation not revolution, for the substance (*Substanz*) of his concrete standpoint is preserved and any new formation must be made to fit the old in every sphere.

The theologian of culture is not held back by such considerations. He stands freely within the living cultural movement, open not only to every other form but also to every new spirit. Of course, he also lives off the soul of a definite concreteness, for one can live only within something concrete, but he is always prepared to expand this concreteness, to change it. As a theologian of culture, he takes no interest in the continuity of the church. To be sure, for this reason, he is also, compared to the church theologian, at a disadvantage, because he is in danger of becoming a fashionable prophet of an essentially doubtful and ambiguous cultural development.

Thus, both are led into a relation where each complements the other. This is best achieved in the unity of a person, although, indeed, this is not something to be desired in all circumstances, for the type of each must be allowed to develop freely. *In any case, a real opposition is no longer possible once the theologian of culture acknowledges the necessity of the concrete standpoint in its continuity and the church theologian acknowledges the relativity of every concrete form with respect to the exclusive absoluteness of the religious principle itself.*

However, the ideal of a theology of culture reaches beyond the distinction between the theology of culture and the theology of the church. This ideal does not, of course, demand a culture in which the polar distinction between sacred and profane has been annulled—for in the world of reflection and abstraction this is impossible—rather it demands a culture in which a unitary substance (*Gehalt*), an immediate and spiritual substance (*Substanz*), is brought to realization throughout the entire cultural movement, a culture that thereby brings to expression an all-comprehending religious spirit whose continuity is identical with the continuity of culture itself. Then, the opposition between the theology of culture and the theology of the church will have been annulled, for such an antithesis is only the expression of a culture that is divided between substance and meaning.

However, even in a new cultural unity, the theologian would be entrusted with the cultivation of the elements of culture that are predominantly religious, and, to be sure, he would do this on the soil of a particular religious community, one that does not really differ from the rest of the cultural community. Rather, just as the pietistic communities liked to characterize themselves as an "ecclesiola in ecclesia," so should the church, from the standpoint of the theology of culture, be an ecclesiola within the ecclesia of the cultural community in general. *The church is, as it were, a circle which, ideally, is entrusted with the task of removing the vital religious elements within the cultural community from chance by creating a specifically religious sphere for them, to gather them and concentrate them, theoretically and practically, and thereby to make them into a powerful, indeed, into the most powerful factor of culture, one that bears all the rest.*

In conclusion, permit me to make a few remarks about the most important bearers of the cultural-theological task: the theological faculties. What is the meaning of the theological faculties and what meaning do they receive in our framework? From the standpoint of science, the theological faculties are justly mistrusted on account of two presuppositions: first, when theology is defined as the scientific knowledge of god interpreted as a particular object among others; second, when theology is conceived as the presentation of a definite limited confession with authoritative claims. In both cases, the autonomy of the other functions is threatened even though all of them go on externally alongside each other. However, a *Universitas litterarum*, conceived as a systematic unity, is then impossible. These objections cease at once, if theology is defined as the normative science of religion and it is made to run parallel with normative ethics, aesthetics, etc., and if it is made clear what "standpoint" means within the context of the cultural sciences, as we did at the outset. The theological faculties, however, not only maintain equal standing among other faculties, but, if we ascend to the cultural-theological standpoint and view them from there, they receive an entirely universal and preeminent cultural significance as do the particular philosophical faculties. Then the theological faculties carry out one of the greatest and most creative tasks within culture. The demand for the removal of the theological faculties arose during the Age of Liberalism, of individualistic and antithetical culture. Socialism took it up, without having examined its enmity to the existing churches. It contradicts its own essence, for its essence is the unity of culture. Of course, it has no place for a hierarchy or theocracy or a religious heteronomy, yet, for its own completion it requires an all-comprehending religious substance that alone, by means of theonomy, can free the autonomy of the individual as well as of the individual cultural functions from their self-consuming isolation. And for this reason, in behalf of the new cultural unity that is arising on socialist soil, we need theological faculties whose primary and basic task is a theology of culture. Theology, which for almost 200 years has been in the unhappy but necessary situation of defending a position that finally is indefensible and which has had to abandon position after position, must once more take the offensive after abandoning the last remaining of its indefensible, culturally heteronomous positions. It must fight under the standard of theonomy, and under this standard it will triumph, not over the autonomy of culture, but over the secularizing, emptying, and ruin of culture that has taken place during the most recent human epoch. It will conquer, for, as Hegel says, religion is the beginning and the end of everything just as it is the center that gives life, soul, and spirit to all things.

Interpretation

0

The title, "Ueber die Idee einer Theologie der Kultur," seems straightforward enough and fitting for the title of a scholarly address, which Tillich's text originally was. Preliminaries are dispensed with and we are introduced directly to the theme: the *idea* of a theology of culture. We expect to hear about a discipline, its aims and method and scope, and our expectations prove true.

Nevertheless, the title is ambiguous. And, it is not all that common a title. Tillich might better and less ambiguously have entitled his address in any of the following ways: "Entwurf einer Theologie der Kultur" (Outline of a Theology of Culture), or "Ideen zur einer Theologie der Kultur" (Ideas or Thoughts Toward a Theology of Culture)—a very suitable title for the founding of a discipline, which is what Tillich hoped to accomplish through his address, or "Ueber die Theologie der Kultur" (Concerning the Theology of Culture)—which is about as straightforward as one can get. Anyone expert in the theory of titles may find this talk about Tillich's title rather silly, and many others may agree. Yet, there is a definite ambiguity in the title, even though one has to look hard to find it and even though, as seems clear, it was not intended by the author. To take note of it and to consider it briefly here, in this preliminary chapter, casts light on what he has written.

The genitive, "of a theology of culture," may be construed in two ways: as an objective genitive or as a genitive of possession. On the first interpretation, the theology of culture is the object of an idea, what the idea is about or its content. On the second interpretation, the idea belongs to the theology of culture; it is what the theology of culture, or the theologian, thinks or thinks about; or better still, the idea that a theology of culture envisions and whose envisioning consummates the science. This is to use 'idea' in a somewhat older, Platonic sense, according to which it means neither a mere concept nor a definition but a transcendent ideal. Kant's "ideal of pure reason"[1] is a good example of this; the ideal is the idea envisioned or imagined in its concreteness and perfection, which is to say, the idea is a world present to thinking not as its mere theoretical object but as its hoped for or expected goal.[2] To avoid ambiguity Tillich might have entitled his address: "Ueber den Begriff and das Ideal einer Theologie der Kultur" (Concerning the Concept and the Ideal of a Theology of Culture), where 'concept' signifies the a priori constitution of any theology of culture, its basic theoretical assumptions, its purely conceptual possibility, and where 'ideal' signifies its speculative goal, its truth (a concrete, fully realized, systematic totality), no less a priori but in a different sense. There is no doubt that Tillich addresses both themes in his text. Their duality is one of his chief concerns.

By admitting this second sense of 'idea' into the title—my guess is that Tillich only intended the first sense—we gain a broader perspective on Tillich's project. What should then enter our horizon are historical archetypes that aid our thinking and give legitimacy to our thoughts about Tillich and his themes. The profoundly historical nature of his thinking, his desire to invoke through his thoughts and words the great thinking of the past, justifies if it does not require that we use these archetypes for their heuristic value.

One ideal that our perspective now takes in is a living figure, the thinker-creator and the model that he contemplates. The picture of the craftsman contemplating the divine idea or archetype so that what he is fashioning or creating may be noble and worthy of praise, "an image of the intelligible," "a visible god, supreme in greatness and excellence, beauty and perfection, a single uniquely created heaven"[3]—this picture has an honorable place in the history of philosophy, although its importance for philosophy has not always been recognized. Nevertheless, it has had its venerable users. Anselm, for one, uses it in his *Proslogion* to clarify the important distinction between thinking about something, about what it is, and thinking that it really exists, a distinction artfully presented that lures us into the web of his famous argument.[4] Plato paid it the highest tribute by adopting it for his great myth of the creation of the world in the *Timaeus*. It is at work here, in Tillich's text.

Consider Plato's divine craftsman: he is, as Gregory Vlastos nicely puts it, "the noblest image of the deity ever projected in classical antiquity," and the significance that Vlastos sees in it also applies here: "it opens the way to a radically new idea of piety for the intellectual which the traditionalists would have thought impious: that of striving for similitude of God." Also relevant is Vlastos' perception of the connection of this figure with the 'philosopher king' of Plato's Republic, a connection that he finds inspiring and yet disquieting.[5] What makes this divine craftsman noble is not only his supreme intelligence (he is reason itself, or *nous* or *Geist* or *mind*) and his skill (he is a consummate artist), but most especially his moral qualities: he is good. That says it all, but in case any would question his motives, then let it be said that "what is good has no particle of envy in it."[6] Because he is without envy, the creator, who also must be supremely happy for he never ceases to contemplate "that which is and never becomes," desires that "all things be as like as himself as possible." Therefore, we may suppose that he does not frivolously create worlds upon worlds out of nothing (an impossibility for those who portray him), but he attends to the matter at hand, material reality, which is in almost total disorder, and from it he fashions a world worthy of praise, a visible god. What seriousness of purpose! What fidelity! Would it not be appropriate to characterize Plato's divine creator as one who is "faithful to the earth"?[7]

It would not be appropriate, because Plato's creator is a god and his attitude towards the earth is not one of fidelity but of benevolence. His fidelity rather is directed to his transcendent and supersensible model, the eternal idea. Nietzsche, to the contrary, has said that god is dead and his place will be taken by the Overman who denies the supersensible and advocates fidelity to earth.

Yet Plato's *Timaeus* is hardly straightforward in its advocacy of transcendence. His bewildering irony, displayed in all of his writing and which, in part, is a function of an intricate pattern of self-reference and self-concealment, makes any unambiguous reading of his texts suspect. This is no reason, however, to suppose that secretly Plato was an atheist, a materialist, and an aristocratic humanist who, fearing persecution for impiety and recognizing the political utility of transcendent fictions and yet being a philosopher committed to truth, employed his consummate art to fashion works that protected him from popular condemnation, served his interests, and satisfied his scruples. Such a view, even if it were coherent, seems patently false. What is more likely is that Plato was serious, very serious, about his intellectual visions of transcendence, also that he was very aware of the uncertainty of them and of the limitations of human understanding to comprehend even their significance. But, he was not uncertain of his art and of its power to transfigure human life and its institutions, noble individuals, and the cosmos itself, in short, of his ability to praise them. What makes Plato of interest to theologians and, generally, to a certain kind of intellectual, who cannot make sense of the world without the thought of transcendence and who, in spite of human folly and wickedness, so abundantly demonstrated everywhere and always, want to praise being and to celebrate life, is that Plato's art provides them with a means to accommodate their aspirations to their doubts without violating either. So long as Plato's works are remembered, the theological tradition will always be very much of a Platonic tradition, and for good reason.[8]

What has this to do with Nietzsche? It was not my idea to bring him in. As we shall see, Tillich invokes him, and precisely in connection with the idea of creation. This radically human principle is determinative of the theologian's self-identity and of the practice of his craft. Therefore, if my claim is true that Plato's divine creator is a historical archetype of Tillich's conception of a theology of culture, then it becomes necessary to show how this fits, in Tillich's thought, with Nietzsche's archetype of an all too human creator. But, it is not hard to imagine how someone attracted by Nietzsche's ideal of the free spirit, who takes it to be a historical truth, who is a committed theologian and in love with philosophy and with the rich abundance of cultural life and a thinker whose thinking is a kind of play of images—and all of these are true of Tillich—would have permitted Plato's visions to enter his thinking and play determinative roles. Whether this is so and how it is so are questions that lead us into the text.

1

According to the title of Tillich's first section, a distinction is to be drawn between philosophy of religion and theology and the relation between them clarified. Tillich does not begin directly with this distinction but approaches it systematically by the method of division. Theology and philosophy of religion are sciences. The implied beginning of Tillich's exposition is science itself or science in general, which falls into two classes: experiential and cultural. The distinction between them is drawn in terms of their contrasting attitudes toward standpoints, their standpoints on standpoints. Among experiential sciences, standpoints must be overcome or superceded; among cultural sciences, standpoints are the heart of the matter. Did Tillich intend this division to comprehend all of the sciences? Yes and no. Yes, insofar as it pertained to the present exposition of the theology of culture. No, on reflection. Logic and mathematics do not seem to fit into either class, and while it would be interesting to conjecture about how Tillich might have conceived them as either experiential or cultural sciences, the results would be merely conjectural and unnecessary in the light of Tillich's later work. Just four years later, in his book *The System of the Sciences*, Tillich developed a tripartite division of the sciences using a different method of derivation—the method of transcendental analysis.[9] This difference in method is worth noting for it brings to light the different currents of tradition that carry along Tillich's thinking, currents that may flow together in the single stream of Tillich's thought but that, in a fundamentally conceptual way, are never united.

The method of division reflects the realistic attitude of classical philosophy. It belongs with a theory of transcendent, purely intelligible, yet mind-independent ideas. Real distinctions among perceived objects are causally dependent upon a real hierarchy of ideas and their nested divisions, upon conceptual distinctions that ultimately are more real than the mundane experiences that reflect them. At the same time, what resists thought and what thought can shape but never altogether transform is also real. The method of transcendental analysis, on the other hand, reflects the epistemological concerns of modern philosophy. Introduced into philosophy by Kant, it applies to the operations of a universal yet finite mind. Its purpose is to determine the proper limits of the mind's cognitive or, more broadly, rational activity. Although the concepts of thiɔ method constitute subjectivity, they are not presumed really to transcend it. The method and its concept are transcendental and formal not transcendent and fully realized. One of the restrictions that follows from this method, which, of course, is the mind's own self-determination, is the prohibition or self-restriction from epistemic claims about objects that transcend the spatio-temporal framework of human sensibility. With the idealization of Kant's critical philosophy by his German successors, the restrictions that Kant carefully observed fall away and radical possibilities present themselves to thought. The least of these is the possibility of transcending the spatio-temporal framework of experience, rather it is the possibility of the mind positing or creating its own objects for subsumption under its own self-designed structures.[10]

At the outset of his address, Tillich seems to employ the older method of division, albeit casually, as a way of getting to his theme and without implying the older realism of transcendent ideas. For his transcendentalism, as we shall see, is an idealized, romanticized, and historicized version of Kant's. Nevertheless, traces of the older transcendent realism of ideas remain and affect his thinking.

Experiential science having been separated and briefly characterized, Tillich now proceeds to define the nature of cultural science per se. A cultural science essentially is a standpoint whose realization occurs in three moments: critical, historical, and normative. Each moment represents a type of cultural science. Philosophy of religion is an instance of the first type; theology, of the third. The relation between them is polar, each separate yet necessarily connected to the other by some principle of reciprocity or correlation. Historical-cultural science mediates between them.

Having found our way, by the method of division, to theology, we may ask just what kind of theology is this? It is a cultural science; but is it theology of culture? Tillich has not yet used the name, except in the title of his discourse, and this is fitting, for the "normative science of religion" is not a science of all of culture but only of one part of it. So it would seem. We must await developments in the next section before we come to recognize that what seems to be a limitation, in fact, is not one at all. At this point in our discussion, then, we are to think of theology as modern theology that thinks of itself as a science, a cultural science, a normative science whose cultural domain is religion. Is this also a theology of the church? Not exactly; it is more academic than churchly. But, this is to anticipate themes that will be discussed in succeeding chapters.

What are we to make of this division of the sciences into cultural and experiential, into *Kulturwissenschaften* and *Erfahrungswissenschaften*,[11] to use Tillich's precise words? Somehow, it does not seem quite right. More appropriate would be a division into natural and cultural sciences, or natural sciences (*Naturwissenschaften*) and human sciences (*Geisteswissenschaften*). This is the division and the terminology[12] that Wilhelm Dilthey uses, and it derives additional dignity by harking back to the ancient opposition of nature and spirit. To suppose that Tillich overlooked this more than commonplace way of putting the distinction is unreasonable. More than likely, he considered it and decided against using it. Why? Dilthey, in his characterization of the distinction between the two classes of science, may provide an answer. He observes that the two realms of nature and spirit, or the physical and the psychical, are not really separate, at least not in mankind, but designate two attitudes toward the same reality: "What is usually separated into physical and mental [*Physiches und Psychiches*] is vitally linked in mankind. For we, ourselves are part of nature and nature is active in our obscure and unconscious instincts; states of mind are constantly expressed in gestures, facial changes and words and have an objective existence in institutions, states, churches and seats of learning; these provide the contexts of history."[13] Perhaps it was for the sake of consistency with this unity of the psychical and the physical, basic to the philosophy of life and to Nietzsche's anthropology, that led Tillich to seek an alternative terminology. For the old ideology of nature and spirit implies a metaphysical dualism. According to this ideology, nature and spirit are entities that are somehow joined in human life but that remain metaphysically distinct and ultimately separable. This dualism is maintained by Kant, although the canons of his critical philosophy permit its use only on the basis of practical and not theoretical principles. Even with this restriction or, perhaps, just because of it—for it permits everything physical to be reduced to mechanical processes—this dualism is alien to Tillich's intentions.

But, there is still another possiblity. A more suitable opposite of experiential science is not cultural science but a priori or eidetic science. This opposition is Husserlian, and it may be that Tillich was acquainted with it.[14] Husserl characterizes experiential sciences as factual sciences (*Tatsachenwissenschaften*), whose founding acts are experiences of concrete and contingent realities; these are contrasted although not theoretically separable from eidetic sciences, which originate in pure conceptual acts and whose objects are pure essences. Now, although Tillich does characterize cultural sciences as a priori and although his construction of the history of culture is a typology that charts the course of historical development according to preestablished dialectical paths, a comparison of Tillich's theory of science with Husserl's does not suggest that Tillich was working out of Husserl's phenomenology. What is more likely is that he used Husserl's term to call attention to the factual nature of the experiential sciences and thereby to highlight the key difference between them and the cultural sciences. And, that is all.[15]

Experiential sciences (or empirical sciences) presuppose and imagine a real world independent of the mind. This objective world, which in itself is one and the same, is, as such, the criterion of truth. Because the aim of science is truth, every element of subjectivity that enters into the representation of the world must be removed or accounted for. For the practitioners of empirical science to succeed in their enterprise, the world must become for them objectively what it is in itself. According to expectation, science progresses toward this goal. This group of sciences is called empirical not because its members necessarily lack any a priori principles—Tillich is vague on this point, but it makes no difference here—but because of their intended object—the real world—and their aim—to represent this world descriptively as it is in itself, that is, to state the facts. No mention is made here of explanation. The facts are always the same. If one states the facts correctly then one's assertions are true; if incorrectly, then they are false. A strict bivalence is to be adhered to. Assertions about the world, which consists of facts, are either true or false. Tillich is not concerned here with the probability of truths and falsehoods, which belongs to the method of empiricism.[16] If there is no adequate correspondence between the world and some claim made about it, then that claim is false. If, in any scientific inquiry, sufficient evidence has not yet been gathered to warrant a true judgment about the world, we may assume with confidence that, because the world remains one and the same, by carefully gathering data and scrupulously sifting out all influences of subjectivity, the truth will become known. This is the principle of scientific progress. From this standpoint, the history of science is the history of the progress of truth over the errors of subjectivity. The ultimate aim of any experiential science is to represent actual states of affairs, whether they be temporally or spatially remote or present, whether they be great or small in the scheme of things. The idea (or, perhaps, the ideology) of empirical science that Tillich presents here is essentially realistic, and the theory of truth is a correspondence theory.

My interpretation of the opening paragraph of this first section is not beyond doubt the right one. There is reason to believe that it ought not to be the right one. The realism represented there is inconsistent with Tillich's idealistic point of view and with his conception of the theology of culture. Nevertheless, in spite of some obscurities, a closer reading of the text does not discredit it nor does it suggest another. His statements are clear enough, and nothing about his tone suggests that we do otherwise than take him at his word. The first sentence tells us that a necessary requirement in experiential or empirical science is to overcome standpoints. The second sentence tells us why. Standpoints are to be overcome because the real world is the criterion of truth. This world is objective, independent of mind. Standpoints are subjective and the source of error. As is clear from the third sentence, standpoints are overcome not by getting rid of them but by deciding which one among a set of possible but contrary standpoints is true, that is, which one represents the world as it actually is. Tillich does not spell out a procedure for deciding this; most likely, he had in mind a standard empirical procedure of observation and, where appropriate, experimentation. Standpoints consist of propositions or statements that presume to represent actual states of affairs. The examples that Tillich gives state facts about particular things. Two of them are negative: Moses did not write the Mosaic books; Paul is not the author of the letter to the Hebrews. The other is a compound proposition affirming one thing and denying another about the disposition of earth in the solar system. He says nothing about the empirical scientific goal of general explanatory laws.[17]

Tillich represents empirical standpoints as existing in pairs, and in his discussion of them, he confuses the logical relations of contrariety and contradiction. The reader, then, should recall that a proposition that, for example, asserts something about the world is either true or false. A proposition and its denial are contradictories: one must be true and the other false. Contradictories come in pairs. Two or more propositions are contraries when and only when no two of them are contradictories and the logical relation among them is such that only one can be true but all can be false. Tillich's intention seems clear: conflicting standpoints are sets of contrary simple or compound propositions. This is not an insignificant point. One of the cardinal principles of realism is that the world may be other than we think it is, that among several competing hypotheses, all may be false. This, of course, injects an element of contingency into empirical science: however we may suppose our world to be, it may always be otherwise. "Of the different suppositions, one or none is true."

This statement was made about the authorship of *Hebrews*, but it is meant to apply generally. The world is vast, the observer is finite, his wealth of observations on which hypotheses are based is meager compared to the uncomprehended manifold, his opportunities few. Even the most persistent observer supposes that there is an unfathomed world beyond the limited mind, yet it is not unfathomable—such is the confidence of science—and it remains the same for all who observe it, so that it is not unreasonable to hope that in the course of human time science will progress, that limited and unreliable standpoints will give way to more comprehensive and objective ones.

It is difficult to abandon the expectation that the dialectical and idealistic Tillich did not intend to annul this domain of empirical science and its realism. In the light of what he projects for the theology of culture, this seems imperative. Not until the last section of the address does he seem to give us license to nourish our expectation. Anticipating that, let us suppose that this was his intention. How might he have done it? He might have begun by arguing that realism, which is a natural presupposition of the practice of empirical science, is inconsistent. For if, as the concept of realism entails, the world might always be other than we judge it to be, even if our judgments are made according to the most scrupulous and persistently self-critical procedures, then what counts as knowledge is always tainted with an element of subjectivity. Knowledge as judgment necessarily has the quality of certainty, which is subjective, but truth is objective. Thus, the pure criterion that would verify this certainty always remains tantalizingly beyond our grasp. But, if realism is inconsistent, then it is false, and Tillich's remark about the progress of science may be taken as ironic: science will decide, but its decisions will never convey the real truth. Yet, this does not make realism any less a natural and even unavoidable supposition of the practice of empirical science, and, hence, merely to judge it false is not sufficient to overcome it. It is overcome only when it is recognized as an indispensable element of a point of view that, in the historical present, at least, has undeniable validity, as is true perhaps even now of scientific realism. Realism, then, is superseded when it is recognized as a moment in scientific consciousness. According to this view, the history of science becomes not the history of errors and the progress toward truth but a history of standpoints. Merely to judge false the attitude of realism implied in the practice of empirical science seems, then, inappropriate and, indeed, futile. Far better to employ the tactic of removing it from the realm of fact, where a rigorous rule of true or false prevails, to the realm of fancy or fiction, or of self-determining spirit, where it may prosper under a more accommodating rule. But this transports us into the realm of the cultural sciences, a realm that now appears complete and without a rival.

In contrast to the experiential sciences, whose objects are not known to be products of thought, the intended object of any cultural science includes the standpoint itself of the systematic thinker. The 'thing itself' or object of this science, however, is not a mere object but a creating subjectivity, which, taken together with its product, is uniquely individual. The systematic thinker, the cultural scientist, is a creator of a world, for, as we shall see, 'standpoint' signifies the envisioning of a world from its creative center. Here, too, an ideal is intended, but unlike the divine craftsman of Plato's *Timaeus* (although, perhaps, more like Plato), the systematic thinker does not have a clear view of absolutely transcendent forms. His ideal is mediated through the historical past. In short, this thinker is not a god, although he is not without divine traits. Like the empirical scientist, who requires the fiction of scientific realism, he may, out of necessity (like the necessity that Kant supposed keeps us thinking transcendental ideas), adhere to the fiction of a transcendent realm of ideas and values; yet, because his scientific attitude involves self-awareness, this adherence cannot be without an element of irony. Whatever illusions the creative thinker may allow himself to have about the universality of his thoughts, he knows himself to be a thoroughly historical being, his thoughts are worldly although self-transcending. Even the theologian, or more precisely what he thinks, has been "brought down from heaven to earth." One is reminded of Zarathustra's appeal that we be faithful to earth. How a theologian is to remain faithful to earth is something that we might hope to find out by reading this address.

If these remarks seem radical, they are no more so than Tillich's initial characterization of the cultural sciences. The standpoint of the thinker-creator is a uniquely individual moment within the history of culture. But the history of culture is not a progressive history, rather it is a dialectical sequence of moments. Historical existence is constituted by cultural acts. History is the realm of being that culture creates. Yet, one might infer from this, it is a realm in which any pretense of thought to pure timeless universality is unmasked. But, Tillich does not mention this pessimistic implication.

In the cultural sciences, then, cognitive and productive thinking converge; not only is the intended object of cultural science objective only so far as it is something made, but knowing and creating are not separate acts. To know a cultural object, one must approach it not objectively, as a fact to be counted or accounted for, but subjectively and creatively, as something to be interpreted. One must draw it up into a new creative figuration that is the standpoint of the creative thinker. Here, then, true or false do not apply, but only, perhaps, an internal validity or rightness. Any inquiry concerning cultural facts belongs to the fiction of the empirical sciences. Here, not realism but a self-sufficient perspectivism prevails. What is realized in the cognitive-creative act of the systematic thinker is a cultural ideal. Cultural ideals are not mere general concepts but norms: dogmatic systems, aesthetic values, moral and social ideals, and so forth. One may well wonder whether there is such a thing as a cultural science as distinct, for example, from artistic production, for Tillich draws no clear distinction between them. Indeed, since there are no timeless universals among the norms of the cultural science and since the semantic values of true and false also do not apply here, one may also wonder whether the system of the sciences envisioned here is not an anarchy of science? This may seem too fanciful in the light of Tillich's later systematic constructions, which are unmistakably hierarchical, but not in the light of what comes later in this address. In Section 4, Tillich speaks approvingly of the paradoxical political form of 'Anarchism', a kind of political Expressionism.

However, one cannot be sure of Tillich's intentions, not the least because his remarks about concepts and universals seem hopelessly obscure. The claim that cultural science cannot make use of universal concepts except ones that are only disguised or concealed concrete norms seems patently false and self-refuting. Surely, the concepts of 'norm' or 'cultural-scientific concept' are universal or general concepts and not norms in the sense that Tillich uses that term here. The claims that a universal concept cannot be derived from a cultural idea (this claim Tillich himself will contradict) and that abstractions cannot facilitate the experience of concrete forms of life or be used to envision the future as hope or expectation, also seem false, if indeed they make any sense at all. Yet, we must try to make something of what is said here, for a theory of concepts or ideas is central to Tillich's project. The best procedure is to begin with some simple observations drawn from what Tillich has written thus far.

First, ideas, or at least those employed in the cultural sciences, are instruments of the life of the mind, which, for their proper employment, do not require any objective reference, that is to say they are not subservient to the process of perception. Second, they seem to be divided into theoretical and practical ideas, or into abstract and concrete, or into universal concepts and norms. For Tillich, the pairs are coextensive if not synonymous. Third, norms or practical ideas are primary in at least three ways: they are first in order of occurrence, thinking begins and acquires its instrumentation in concrete experience; they are primary in some epistemic sense as the most authoritative and the richest conveyors of meaning; they are primary in the metaphysics of the person, the individual becomes a person by having such ideas, that is, by originating them for himself and by fashioning and interpreting his own existence in terms of them, for the basic function of norms is to set goals for the conduct of life lived within the framework of an envisioned world, that is, lived meaningfully. Cultural ideas, therefore, broadly speaking, are moral. General, theoretical concepts are secondary. They are derived by abstracting from concrete norms or, perhaps, from experience in general. Abstraction proceeds by "nullifying" the concreteness of the norm. Yet, concreteness is the essence of an idea.

Thus, abstract concepts must recall some essence, some founding personal experience, if they are to be made capable of any use at all. Fourth, ideas originate spontaneously, although not arbitrarily and not without antecedents, from the creative synthetic acts of individuals. In short, they are the work of genius. The products of genius are unique (exemplary but inimitable) yet universal. Their universality is not to be confused with the generality of a theoretical concept, rather it is the universality of approbation. Approbation or praise is a judgment about a particular in which everyone should join.[18] Still to be made clear is what Tillich means by 'concrete'. Not surprisingly, since he is well aware of its Hegelian uses,[19] it means something actual, a fully realized mature individual, but also something historical and not merely natural, hence, something unique, free, and unfathomable. 'Historical' signifies not merely something present or past, but an actual life that, as it were, opens up the future, an exemplary being having the quality of a universal that is not abstract. A fully realized self-interpreted human life is exemplary, it is historically self-transcending because the fullness of its meaning extends beyond its physical presence. It becomes the ideal, the archetype or model for the cultivation of life and the embodiment of all cultural ideas. All cultural concepts, then, are normative concepts that originate in creation.

This brief outline, however, does not include everything that counts as an idea or concept in Tillich's system. Most notably, what is lacking are categories, pure a priori concepts that have a prominent place in the outline of a system of the cultural sciences about to be presented. Second, and this is fundamental to the theme of this essay, it must be made clear how among the various ideas available to the creative thinker for the founding of a standpoint, some are so drawn together in the act of creation that they attain the dignity of theology. These issues must await further development of the concept of standpoint.

I have said that Tillich's theory of cultural science is a perspectival one, whose object is not some real entity independent of any point of view but one that takes in the perspective itself. A perspective or standpoint is the self-positing expression of a creative individual. A system of the sciences is now to be derived from this creative act. First, we note that it is not the individual alone who creates. Tillich takes it to be a necessary condition of the act of cultural creation that the agent belong to a circle, a society of persons whose relation is so intimate that the circle itself may be said, more or less, to have committed the act of creation. The center of cultural creation, the standpoint, is itself a circle. Yet, this circle of persons is represented by an individual. An individual expresses the standpoint. Moreover, the standpoint is not an isolated place or moment, its definiteness and completeness is in part a function of its ability to take in what encircles it. Tillich likens the creative standpoint to an ever-expanding horizon of circles beyond circles of culture. Its horizon is the cultural world, present and past: communities, cultural domains, institutions, traditions, texts, works of art and their varied fates, systems of thought, constitutions, manifestos, and so forth. Hegel's objective spirit is invoked here, but the reference is not intended to send us back to Hegel's *Encyclopedia* for a clue or fundamental insight. Tillich's use of the term 'objective spirit' is broader than Hegel's.[20] It is synonymous with culture itself. Dilthey's definition seems more cogent:

> [By objective spirit] I understand the manifold forms in which what is shared in common by individuals in the realm of meaning attains to objectivity. In this objective spirit, the past is for us a continuously enduring present. Its sphere extends from the style of life, the forms of commerce to the framework of purposes that society has formed for itself, to morals, justice, the state, religion, art, science, and philosophy. For even the work of genius represents a common endowment of ideas, of the inner life and of ideality in a certain time and environment.[21]

These encirclements, then, do not make the act of creation any less individual or heroic. They signify, rather, that an individual who lacks a cultural memory and who is cut off altogether from contemporary cultural life can only act willfully and arbitrarily, never creatively.

In this setting, the act of creation occurs. It is a single act with three moments. The creator, encircled, surveys, from his finite historical standpoint, the cultural world. The creator is the standpoint personified, whose first act is to derive from the domains of objective spirit, its "mother soil," the "universal forms of spiritual reality." This is the first moment in the act of cultural creation. What does Tillich mean by these universal forms, whose derivation is the initial creative act? Does he mean the forms or domains or general classes of cultural life: art, religion, morality, and so forth? Or, does he mean the concepts and categories that constitute any cultural reality as such, a kind of 'first philosophy' of culture? From what follows, it is clear that he means the latter. An account of these categories and their derivation must await completion of the presentation of the act of creation. We come now to the second moment of creation. The standpoint, like Emerson's eyeball, surveys its surroundings starting from its outermost horizon. Beginning from there and moving inward through ever narrowing circles, it takes in the "historical endowments of concrete spirituality," that is, the cultural heritage, and thereby it discovers its own concrete limitation. This second moment is an act of historical self-definition and of self-justification. Self-definition of the standpoint is an act of historical construction, not a mere chronicle of cultural history from past to present but a philosophical history, a narrative of a necessary sequence of cultural moments, much like, one might suppose, what is to be found in Hegel's lectures on art, religion, philosophy, and on history itself, but more personal. The necessity of this sequence may be the working out of a hidden purpose or fate, but so far as it is something that can be grasped or understood, the form of this necessity is derived from the universal forms of spirit, the categories or concepts, as it were, schematized in time. Justification, which is self-justification of the standpoint, then may be taken to be the representation of this necessity. Providence or the self-realization of spirit are two interpretations of this necessity; so is Nietzsche's doctrine of eternal recurrence. These do not exhaust the possibilities, and none of these is necessarily implied here. The second moment of self-definition reaches its conclusion in self-positing, which is the third and final moment, the climax of the act of creation: "in a creative self-positing act, [the personified standpoint] fashions a new, individual and unique synthesis of universal form and concrete content." 'Self-positing' is Fichte's term and was used by him to signify the origination of the absolute self, which is the principle of his system of idealism.[22] Here, it means the self-realization of the historical person, who is in this case finite yet infused with something like an absolute power, "the power of the concrete," and who, by this power, creates out of the past a new world and thereby becomes a person, unique, concrete, and fully formed. Finally, an analysis of the creative act introduces a trio of cultural sciences: the philosophy of culture, which considers the universal a priori forms of culture; a philosophy of the history of culture, which is most concerned with cultural values or norms and which is a transitional discipline, moving through a historical construction from the universal to the unique that locates and justifies the standpoint; and a normative science of culture, a normative-systematic construction of the cultural present, which is the standpoint itself.

With the aid of this construction, theology can be located among the cultural sciences, and philosophy of religion also, for the reader should be reminded that the aim of this first section is to define the relation between theology and the philosophy of religion. Without comment, we find ourselves removed from the universal dominion of culture and placed, as it were, among its various provinces, as though all talk about universal cultural science were merely talk about culture in general, a kind of 'meta-talk' that describes the general framework of the discussion of cultural science. Its work done, this voice becomes silent, and we hear only voices coming from the various spheres of culture. The way to theology, then, is prepared by a set of examples. The examples given are art and morality. Philosophy of art is a critical and phenomenological account of the essences and values peculiar to the domain of art. This is to be distinguished from aesthetics, which judges how these values and essences apply to objects.[23] Likewise, moral philosophy is to be distinguished from normative ethics. And, likewise, philosophy of religion is to be distinguished from theology, which is "the concrete normative science of religion." This, Tillich insists, is the only scientifically useful concept of theology. In any other sense, theology would not be a science.

But, one may ask, just what is theology about? The answer is "Norms." Norms are the expression of the dominion of a standpoint in a particular sphere of culture. Is theology about anything more? Tillich answers "No." Indeed, he responds with a twofold denial. The justification of both denials may be presented as follows:

(1) A cultural science has no object other than its own standpoint and the concepts and norms that are constitutive of it.[24]

(2) Theology is a (concrete, systematic, normative) cultural science.

(3) Therefore, theology has no object other than its own standpoint.

Theology, then, is not about god and it is not about revelation, if these are taken to be real, extramental objects and not merely expressions of a standpoint. They are admitted to theology's domain only as part of its conceptual scheme, as meanings. It should be clear that Tillich's argument, if sound, entails the rejection of realism and transcendence in theology. The argument is valid. Are the premises true? Yes, in a certain sense. More precisely, within the framework of cultural science, they are valid. For the establishment of this framework, we must return to Kant. On the basis of the self-limitation of reason through the critical philosophy, Kant has shown the impossibility of theistic proofs and speculative theology, in general. In this way, he has "brought theology down from heaven to earth" and changed it into a regulative or normative science.[25] Thus, on the basis of this construction of theology, it is no longer possible to claim that theology's concepts correspond to real entities. Those concepts of rational theology: a perfect being, a first cause and author of existence, and so forth, that arise in the human mind may still be employed immanently as means of bringing unity to the sum of our knowledge and meaning to our normative constructions. But, beyond that, their employment is illusion. In this sense, theology has been brought down to earth and confined to a world. It now becomes a cultural science, limiting those who practice it to the search for unitary constructions of the mind's contents, carried along by the currents of the history of the life of the mind. A more radical way of putting Tillich's construction is to declare that god is dead but his idea has been reborn in the mind of the creative individual. From the new standpoint of theology, the standpoint whose ground is Hegel's objective spirit, the theologian realizes Nietzsche's concept of human creativity.[26] Theology brought down to earth is not confined to a merely regulative role but is liberated and made creative.

Justification of the rejection of a supernatural and, hence, objective revelation comes also from the 'wave' of insights gained from the historical study of religion, insights doubtless derived not only from the historical study of Christianity—the development of dogma and cultus, the formation of the biblical books and the canon, and of ecclesiastical offices and social organization—but also from the historical and comparative study of the great religious traditions that make claims about the absoluteness of Christianity and its supernatural origin problematic. He also cites the critique of supernaturalism both from a logical and religious, that is, prophetic, point of view.

Theology, then, is not supernatural. The theologian does not go beyond his own standpoint in search of an object for his science. Indeed, in the very process of self-definition and self-justification accomplished by the construction of a philosophy of the history of the past that encircles him, the theologian 'breaks through' those circles of the past whose authority has taken on the aspect of the supernatural. By this expression I take Tillich to mean that the supernatural wineskins of scripture, sacred office, orthodoxy, and similar sacred institutions have been burst by the new wine of the secular art of philosophical history, just as, in Expressionist art, the creative power of abstract form breaks through the forms of everyday vision (see Chapter 4). This new wine, however, is not solely reason's vintage. Tillich hastens to add that the new theology is not the old rational theology in disguise. It is not, for example, as in the case of Kant, merely instrumental to the moral life, which in turn is subject entirely to the autonomous rational will, nor is it, as Hegel supposed it, merely the external expression of the internal movements of speculative reason. What makes theology more than rational is its historicalness. There seems a strange paradox here, for it would appear as though the rational arguments and critiques, which circumscribe theology and belong to its standpoint, are subject to a nonrational fate that affects not their logical integrity but their cogency. The paradox is made acceptable, however, if one thinks of the theologian-thinker-creator as a genius whose production, a new standpoint—which is a world, a form of life—may contain the most rational of elements, but that combines them in a totality that includes much more: a sense of the sublime, feelings of earthly delight, moral grace, poetry, and art. These constitute a world viewed by the spirit's eye, a world that is judged good or praised, not in an act of theoretical understanding but in something like aesthetic judgment.[27] The rule or norm of this judgment does not precede the creative acts of envisioning or judging the world (they are basically identical acts) but originates in the act itself. A norm is not like a rule that one follows in playing a game, rather it is like the highest skill exhibited in playing it well. To such high skill we may attribute the origin of the game itself.

Thus far, Tillich has attended only to the nature of theology as a cultural science. He now turns to the relation between theology and philosophy of religion. His brief remarks on this theme, which conclude the first section of his address, will evoke more lengthy comments that will bring us back, finally, to a brief review of his theory of ideas.

Although the theme is the relation between theology and philosophy of religion, in treating it, Tillich returns once more to the general relation between "philosophy of culture and the normative systematics of culture." Why he chooses to treat his subject in this way is not clear to me. Perhaps, it is because he believes that the relation between theology and philosophy of religion is the same as the relation between every pair of cultural sciences, the same as that between the philosophy of art and aesthetics and between moral philosophy and normative ethics. Perhaps, it is because he believes that in every instance, normative science is theological. Perhaps, both. In any case, the latter is true of church theology, at least according to its ideal, which it more closely approximated before its authority was challenged by secular culture. These are issues that will come up in subsequent chapters.

The relation between philosophy and normative systematics, and between philosophy of religion and theology, is one of correlation. The meaning of this term, which has become almost the trademark of Tillichean theology, requires more than a cursory exposition. What does Tillich mean here by 'correlation' (*Wechselwirkung*)? In the light of the exposition up to this point, it may seem natural to expect to discover its meaning in the relation between concepts and norms. However, Tillich tells us that it is not to be found here, and yet, in the very next paragraph, the last of this section, summing up in a grand manner and in apparent self-contradiction to what he said in the previous paragraph, he characterizes the relation between philosophy and theology as a correlation of concepts. Therefore, it seems not inappropriate to begin this exposition of the meaning of correlation by examining the relation between the respective concepts of philosophy and normative science.

Thus far, universal concepts, the concepts of philosophy, have been described as abstractions, which are formed by drawing away from the concrete presentation of an object what ordinarily are assumed to be any nonessential characteristics. Yet, as we have seen, what is essential to a cultural object is just its concreteness. Therefore, universal concepts necessarily fail to represent what a thing is essentially. They are empty, whereas norms, themselves concrete cultural objects, are full. If this is so, then universal concepts lack the capability of doing what they are supposed to do, namely, of representing things to the mind. They convey to consciousness only their empty selves. If, however, we discover in them disguised norms, then they become useful. Abstracting, then, is a kind of concealing whereby a norm is clothed in generality, so that what remains is a cipher for a creative expression. But, then, all genuine thinking must become normative thinking, and theoretical and normative concepts converge. But, if they converge, there is no longer any need of correlation. Correlation presupposes duality and separateness and a tension between opposites. Let us try again and consider correlation as a general relation between abstractions and concretions, between concepts and the concrete representations of things subsumed under the concept. There is certainly reciprocity here and it is not unproblematic, for it is not altogether clear just how concepts come to fit their contents. Nevertheless, reciprocity is a fairly prosaic relation, and it does not fit the heightened sense that Tillich applies to the term 'correlation'. Moreover, there is no sense here of any opposition that correlation is supposed to overcome.

One cannot help thinking that Tillich's reflections may result, at least in part, from a misreading of the problem of abstraction. I am reminded of Hume's theory of abstract ideas.[28] Hume, following Berkeley, developed his theory of abstractions to resolve a contemporary dispute over how abstract or general ideas are thought: when we think of an object in general, for example, man, it is not possible that our thinking take in every possible particular shape and form of man (this would require an infinite mind, if indeed it is thinkable at all); on the other hand, Hume contends, it is just as impossible when we think abstractly to think of an object with no particular quality, to think of it as mere form. What in fact occurs is that whenever we think of an object in general we represent it to ourselves concretely; we do not, to use Hume's example, think of whiteness or roundness but of a white marble sphere, yet because we recall other percepts, a black sphere or a white cube, and note the similarities and differences between them, we are able, by a distinction of reason, to separate them tacitly, and in this way we think abstractly. While reference to Hume may seem farfetched, his theory does involve a kind of correlation. But, clearly, something more is at work here.

Perhaps, an example will aid us in our search for Tillich's concept of correlation. Consider his concept of theology. First of all, there is theology itself, which is not a science with an object other than itself but a concrete cultural standpoint. Second, there is the abstract concept, 'theology', which takes in, indifferently, any of the historical standpoints that may be called 'theological'. Let us include in this class only those great theological standpoints, those associated with great figures of the theological past or their works: one might include in a short list Origen, Augustine, Thomas Aquinas, Calvin, Schleiermacher, or, perhaps, one or more of their writings that have had a profound effect on the development of the theological tradition. Let us consider, finally, those concepts that determine what is needed for a theological standpoint. Theology as norm is an idea of what ought to be, a particular cultural ideal, for example, that every significant human action ought to reflect the perfection of god. This norm is properly understood only when it is experienced concretely (or, perhaps, existentially) as an urgent demand or as a goal to be pursued steadfastly. On the other hand, the abstract concept, 'theology', takes in theological existence wherever it is manifest. What counts as theological is any cultural object that possesses certain properties judged, by abstraction or by the distinction of reason, to be theological properties. These properties are derived from resemblances among objects that, in a preliminary way, have been taken to be theological. One might even call them categories. Here, we may detect an opposition between a norm and an abstract concept. An abstract concept is indifferent to value, to the exemplary value peculiar to a norm. Abstraction may be interpreted as a kind of secular leveling of all cultural formations. Because abstraction would reduce objects to their most common resemblances, it groups together theology's creative exemplars with secondary or derivative figures and with figures of reaction: the work of successors and imitators together with the products of creators, those who codify, rationalize, and conventionalize; who externalize creative thinking by transforming it into systems of rules or right beliefs that can be followed unthinkingly together with genuine creators. But, surely, this is not the fault of the logical procedure of abstraction but of something else for which the term 'abstraction' figuratively stands. Even such deformations can be understood abstractly.

Having been forewarned by Tillich that we shall not find the principle of correlation in the relation between concepts and norms and having confirmed this for ourselves, we must search elsewhere for it. Here, it should occur to us that concepts and norms stand metonymously for standpoints. Not ideas or concepts but standpoints are in correlation. And, standpoints are greater than the concepts that constitute them, for a standpoint first of all is the creative power that fashions concepts into worlds, endowing them with concreteness and normative force. Philosophy of religion and theology, philosophy and the normative-cultural sciences "stand in correlation," each is oriented to the other, that is, looks to and takes its bearings from the other. In every cultural domain, two cultural-scientific standpoints, one theoretical, the other normative, are in correlation. Together, they make up the self-consciousness of that cultural domain. Tillich's characterization of correlation as dialectical may be taken to mean that it is a necessary relation between polar standpoints, by which each member is bound to the other, and that it involves overcoming but not altogether doing away with an opposition that exists between them. What more specifically can be said about it? What, in particular, is the nature of this mutual bond? What does the metaphor of orientation involve with respect to these sciences? Why is something like orientation required? If we imagine the activity of thought as wandering or travelling, then each science may be said to require the other to measure its progress or its deviation. Sciences may be said to measure their progress in terms of their goals, and a science without a goal, or without one that is clearly defined, may be said to be aimless or lost. But, merely to have a goal is not enough, if a science lacks a method and a clear definition of its subject and what counts for it. Perhaps, Aristotle can help us here. Each polar standpoint may be said to require a principle or *arche* that the other has and without which it is incomplete, and yet it cannot have this principle in itself but only through the other. (If orientation is our guiding metaphor here, then, one might argue that orientation requires a point that is fixed and apart from what is to be oriented.) Philosophy or the theoretical standpoint lacks a final cause or goal; the normative standpoint lacks a formal cause. Theology (and normative-cultural sciences generally), then, may be said to imply philosophy of religion (and cultural philosophies generally), because its self-orientation necessarily involves thinking of itself in terms of the concepts that constitute it, that make it a knowable object and hence something capable of self-reflection; and philosophy of religion might be said to imply theology, for if its aim is to become a form of life, then it requires some concrete goal or ideal for which to aim and from which it may guide its progress. Still, one might ask, must philosophy of religion look to theology as its goal? Is it not just as possible, under the general principle of correlation, that philosophy of religion would correlate with a normative-philosophical anthropology or with a form of philosophical theology altogether free of commitments to any historical-religious tradition? Hume's *Natural History of Religion* is a good example of both alternatives. It would appear, then, that while theology is bound to philosophy, that is, to a purely theoretical counterpart that it depends upon if it is to be a science, if it is to think of itself constitutively, philosophy, on the other hand, while bound to some normative science, has several options from which to choose of which theology is only one.

Turning once more to the text, however, we find that Tillich presents us with another interpretation that is at least metaphorically different. We are to imagine philosophy and theology as two standpoints that occupy the same ground. Materially, they are the same standpoint, but each, rather than looking toward the other, looks in a different direction. Philosophy may be imagined to look to the conceptual ground beneath the standpoint, theology to the ideal heaven above. Each has its own work that involves producing ideas and concepts, which, of course, is the work of establishing and maintaining their respective standpoints. "Philosophy works out universal, a priori, and categorial concepts on the broadest empirical basis and in systematic relation with other values and concepts of essence. The normative sciences work up the special content and the principles that determine value into special systems for every cultural science."

So far, the image does not yet convey a sense of correlation but merely of situational identity, so to speak. This comes immediately, in the next paragraph. By means of its own work, each standpoint nourishes the other. From the result of the work of the cultural sciences, philosophy's universal concepts derive richness and vitality. From the work of philosophy, or at least its fashioning of a "highest universal concept" that, thanks to the cultural sciences has attained a "comprehensive fullness," the cultural sciences receive the dignity of science. It seems fair to infer that the exchange between philosophy and the cultural sciences is mediated through the common soil that both stand upon or are rooted in. It should be noted with respect to this depiction of correlation that the correlates are defined somewhat differently. On the one side, there is philosophy, whose task seems to be to develop universal concepts or one highest concept for all of the domains of culture, and on the other side, there is a manifold of normative-cultural sciences. Are we to suppose that there is just one philosophy of culture, or as was suggested earlier, does Tillich envision a kind of first philosophy of culture, to be supplemented by numerous special philosophies for the various cultural domains, one of which is the philosophy of religion? Also noteworthy is the curious conception of the a priori presented here. Are categories a priori in a critical sense of that expression, as the necessary antecedents of experience, or are they the most general empirical concepts whose formation requires that we work from the broadest possible empirical, and in the case of cultural sciences, historical base, or is, perhaps, a third position intended?[29] And, then, what is the relation of the categories to the objective spirit, the mother soil, from which they are to be derived? I think it is safe to rule out an empiricist interpretation of Tillich's theory of the categories and to take his mention of an empirical base to be his recognition that the function of categories is to make our experiences intelligible. More than likely. Tillich's conception of the a priori is transcendental although not transcendent. The mother soil of objective spirit is contained within and fashioned by a universal self-validating reason.[30]

Assuming that the metaphorical difference between these two depictions of correlation—one calling for theoretical and normative science to look away from each other while each secretly nourishes the other, the other that has each take its bearing from the other—does not imply a conceptual difference or, worse, an inconsistency, one may still wonder why such elaborate talk is needed to convey what seems to be a simple truth about science, namely, that in every case, one should always know what one's scientific work is about and what it is after, and why we should think of these two simple questions in terms of polarity and dialectic and correlation. Just what is Tillich up to? It is too early in this exposition to answer this question, which is of fundamental importance. The answer that comes most immediately to mind and that, I think, will prove to be the right one, is that Tillich is trying to find a place for theology among the secular sciences, but this is only a stage on the way to an unstated goal to restore theology to preeminence among the sciences. Whether this is his intention, and whether it is a wise one or wisely executed by him are questions whose more definitive and complete answers must await the conclusion of this interpretation.

Setting aside the question of the relation of philosophy and theology for the moment, I return finally to Tillich's theory of ideas. His characterization of philosophy in general as a critical-cultural theoretical science implies that, in his scheme of things, there are categories, that is, pure, a priori concepts. While they may be derived by abstraction, they are not merely residual—what remains after content is carefully removed by thought from a set of similar perceptions—rather, they are the foundational elements of consciousness, but of a human consciousness thoroughly embedded in history. Among a priori concepts, Tillich includes not only categories, although these are basic, but also essences and values. These together constitute the systematic framework of scientific experience generally.

As mere forms, to be sure, they are useless unless they are interpreted as forms of possible concrete experience. To disregard this use and to consider only their formal relations is mere conceptual play, mere formalism.[31] Tillich seems to think that a priori concepts are derived from some foundational cultural experience, a kind of basic intuition of reality. Hence, they are always related to norms but logically are independent of them. But this implies a theory of categorial pluralism, for on the basis of his theory of cultural science, there could be many indeed an unlimited number of sets of categories, essences, and values, as many as there are cultural domains. Only if one founding cultural experience were to be discovered to stand out among all the rest and only if it were to differ from all the rest in some discernible way that not only sets it apart from them but shows it to be more basic, ultimately basic, in some metaphysical sense of the term, could we posit both a truly universal cultural norm and a truly universal conceptual scheme. In the closing paragraph of the section Tillich alludes to this. The "highest universal concept," which is undoubtedly the concept of being, derives its encompassing force, that is, its power to be universal, from a concrete realization, a normative standpoint, that in turn receives from this concept the dignity of a scientific standpoint. What is this founding experience? Perhaps, it is the experience of an absolute limit to thought.[32] In this connection, the concept of being is not so much a category to be applied to some possible object of experience but a rather uniquely universal concept (neither category—unless it be designated the supreme category—nor value nor essence) whose only possible object of experience is the limit of experience itself. It is, thus, a boundary concept, a principle that causes us to ask what the totality of experience might mean. If there is such a founding experience and if it is from it that the concept of being originates and, hence, ontology, which here must be a first philosophy of culture, then it is not hard to see how its normative counterpart might claim for itself the dignity of theology. And this I shall take as the answer to my earlier question.

Finally, then, a brief summary of Tillich's categorial scheme. He posits three categories: substance, form, and content. These are the categories of the possibility of cultural experience, indeed of all experience, for, as Tillich will argue in the last section of his address, all human experience, that is, all consciousness that is interpretable, is part of culture. Substance stands apart and transcends the other two. This is the 'highest concept' that Tillich refers to in the final paragraph of this section; it might be characterized as the pure being of meaning. In German his terms are *Gehalt* and *Substanz;* the latter he uses only once, the former, generally throughout. I translate both as substance.[33] We should think of substance here not in an Aristotelian sense, as something that is in a primary sense, something that exists in its own right in contrast to the properties of a thing. Rather, we should think of it more Spinozistically, as a unique and metaphysically ultimate reality, which is the infinite ground of all existence. But, we must modify it further in a radical way: we must think of it in a Kantian sense as a category, as the fundamental and ultimate category of meaning, the grounding principle of consciousness. If, further, we think of this principle in a romantic mood, as more unfathomable than comprehensible, as more like nothing than something to the finite rational mind when it approaches this ultimate mystery, then, I believe, we will have it precisely. Tillich, after all, was a romantic idealist.

2

The second section of Tillich's address is transitional. It is supposed to take us from 'systematic theology', which here is a theology of the church, to the theology of culture. First, Tillich will show why it is necessary to take leave of church theology. Second, he will explain why this leave-taking does not involve taking leave of theology. Indeed, he will argue that a theology of culture not only remains a possibility for the errant theologian but a necessity for culture itself.

The theologian must take leave of church theology, because the church has lost its right of universal authority over the spheres of human culture. As a cultural domain, the church has become empty, its rights and privileges, never rightfully its own, having been secured by several autonomous domains of secular culture. It is left only with its dogma, which, we may suppose, the world does not want. A theology with only dogma would hardly seem to qualify as a science. Tillich does not say this, but it is easy to imagine that he wanted his readers to draw this judgment, for his silence over the possibility that theology might continue to prosper in the modern age as church dogmatics, perhaps assisted by apologetics, seems to be a silence of condemnation. And, Tillich's silence about apologetics after mentioning it offhand as a modern addition to the traditional content of theology seems even more a condemning silence. One cannot, however, hold back the question why theology of culture should not be taken as a kind of apologetics. This silence about apologetics is puzzling, because, later, Tillich, although recognizing the impropriety of certain kinds of apologetics and acknowledging that the term "has fallen into disrepute," does not hesitate to characterize his entire theological program as apologetics; and, just prior to the first World War, he developed a program of 'Church Apologetics' that anticipated the theology of culture.[34] The solution to this puzzle awaits the next step in this development of the concept of the theology of culture.

Theology of culture is the successor not of dogmatics and not of apologetics, as practiced by modern theology—should we read 'modern' ironically?—it is the successor to theological ethics. Why theological ethics? The answer, I believe, should reflect the character of modern theology since Schleiermacher.[35] The relation of the theologian to his subject is not a purely theoretical one, his first concern is not with a body of dogma but with a human community, a church. Therefore, it is primarily a moral relationship. Hence, not dogma but ethics is fundamental to the church's life. Dogma, properly understood, reflects the ethical life of the church. But, if the church's life is to be understood, if its character and purpose are to be set forth clearly for the guidance and direction of this community, which is the task of the theologian as a 'prince of the church', then not dogmatics but theological ethics is the primary theological discipline.[36] Theological ethics, however, is a normative science and, as such, according to Tillich's system of the sciences, must have a philosophical counterpart, and it is just this characteristic of theological ethics that points the theologian beyond the church and this looking beyond is what renders doubtful the claim of theological ethics to be a science. A critical examination of theological ethics leaves the theologian caught in a dilemma: either he remains within the church, in which case what he does is without all validity as science, or he leaves the church, in which case he no longer does theology. He must choose between piety or secular science.

But why can't theological ethics remain a church theology and at the same time claim for itself the role of a normative ethics? This would give it a place among the sciences according to the construction just presented. And, what is more, although Tillich does not mention this argument, correlation with philosophical ethics would provide the church with a new constitution, more fitting for its role in secular society—this clearly is

what Schleiermacher hoped for, and this hope has not gone unfulfilled. There need be no conflict with philosophical ethics, because the latter is not concerned about moral norms but only
with the essence of morality. Does this not point the way to a
justification of theological ethics as a cultural science, or is it only
a rationalization? Tillich seems to suggest that it is the latter.
Why? His response is another question: "Why should normative
ethics be theological?" He assumes, correctly (as, of course, did
Schleiermacher), that there can be no essential difference between ethics and theological or religious ethics, so that, although
theology in general is the normative science of religion, theological ethics is not just the normative science of religious ethics
but of ethics as such, and therefore, if it is to be a cultural science,
it must take moral philosophy as its correlate. However, if we
take the standpoint of moral philosophy, there seems no reason
why it must have its correlate in theology. Moral philosophy
must have a normative correlate, but, Tillich argues in its behalf,
it has the right to choose its own correlate, and this right must not
be taken from it.[37] This right, we shall see later, is not claimed
arbitrarily but resides in the autonomous constitution of moral
philosophy. If moral philosophy should decide, on the basis of
principles not yet identified, to be in correlation with a non-
theological normative ethics, and if theological ethics should persist in its claim to be normative ethics, and if we should grant
validity to both claims, it should be made clear that we thereby
have allowed the pernicious doctrine of twofold truth to enter the
sphere of ethics. But this doctrine is evidently false. Indeed, consciousness cannot even tolerate it. We then must choose between
theological and secular normative ethics. But, on what grounds
can a choice be made? At this point, it should be recalled that the
justification of a normative-cultural science involves a historical
construction, and this means that justification is always tempo-
rary, bound to some moment in history. What was once a justified normative standpoint may be so no longer. The case of theological ethics can be made by appealing to its concreteness and
historical continuity and to its more immediate availability to the
ethical life. The ethical life requires a concrete environment if it is
to be fully realized, that is, a community encircled by traditions

and long-established sentiments. The church exemplifies such a community. Thus, normative ethics is properly theological because moral realization can take place only within the church. This claim was once justified and its justification continued as long as the church, as a social institution, exercised authority over all of the domains of culture or, at least, over those social institutions that belong most directly to the ethical life: the family, the community, and the nation. But, this is no longer the case. In protestant countries, and particularly in Germany, the church has long since ceased to exercise or to claim for itself such authority. The church has been displaced by a dominant secular community and by communities in every cultural domain. In the present, therefore, the claim of theological ethics is no longer justified, and the awareness of this fact belongs to the historical self-awareness of the modern church. Theological ethics has become a curiosity, like "German, or Aryan, or bourgeois ethics, aesthetics, science, or sociology." Even these may have their adherents, but this does not make them any less curiosities, which are not to be taken seriously by the honest thinker.

Although theological ethics has lost its validity as a science, one must not fault its intention. This intention is now taken over by theology of culture, which alone can promise its fulfillment. What is this intention? Why is it still valid? And what capability does the theology of culture have that justifies Tillich's claim? The answer to the first question may go something like this: theological ethics was supposed to establish the moral authority of the church over all of the domains of culture and over all human communities. This intention is still valid, because human society and its culture would otherwise lack unity. Culture, in this instance, may be interpreted as involved in shaping the self-consciousness of a community, giving it self-identity and meaning and purpose. Perhaps, we will gain a better understanding of what Tillich means by the intention of theological ethics if we consider some historical antecedents. It is clear that the scope of theological ethics, as Tillich understands it, takes in not merely personal ethics but social ethics as well, and the term 'social' should apply here to the polis as well as to other social groups, such as the family and the local community. Thus, the scope of theological ethics is equivalent to the scope of politics as Aristotle conceived it, of the highest good that served the whole of human life, or of Plato's ideal of justice and its embodiment in the best regime, the Republic. The latter seems especially appropriate, for, as we have seen, what gives the dignity of theology to a cultural science is its correlation with the highest idea. Theology of culture is able to fulfill this highest intention of theological ethics because it does not stand as one among the many sciences, because, through its connection with the highest or deepest principle, it is above and below them all. Theology of culture is still the normative science of religion, but the cultural domain of religion has opened up and taken in the rest. This, of course, is only an ideal, but nevertheless, one that is supposed to be determinant of human consciousness. And, is the theologian of culture a modern philosopher king and not just a prince of the church? With this thought, one may begin to feel the same disquiet that troubled Vlastos.

Now the puzzle introduced previously finds its solution. Tillich uses theological ethics and not apologetics as the vehicle that will take the theologian out of the church and into society to find his calling, because it is not his intention—Tillich's and the cultural theologian's—merely to defend the church from secular assault while reforming it from within but of leaving the church in order to rediscover or refound it outside of its historical boundaries.[38]

The disquiet just mentioned is fed by what appears to me to be a shift in Tillich's attitude toward normative-cultural sciences, as they were presented in the previous section. There, Tillich seemed to be guided by the thought of a creative anarchy among the cultural sciences. This anarchy is not mere disorder but a self-ordering form of human community. Among them, true and false did not apply. Yet, here, Tillich rejects the possibility of more than one normative science of ethics because it seems to require admission of the doctrine of twofold truth. This doctrine was apparently devised during the Middle Ages to accommodate the incompatability between certain claims of natural philosophy and Christian doctrine about the eternity of the world, the immortality of the soul, divine providence, and other topics common to

philosophy and theology.[39] The doctrine provided a way of separating contradictory claims—for example, that the world has a
beginning or has no beginning but is eternal, that the soul is an
immortal substance or is the form of the body that dissolves at
death—by limiting their validity to their own theoretical and
doctrinal frameworks. This version of the doctrine is not unlike
Tillich's cultural-scientific doctrine of multiple standpoints. A
stronger version of the doctrine, one that would attribute truth to
contradictory claims, is obviously intolerable. This clearly is the
version that Tillich has in mind. He is denying the validity of more
than one normative standpoint in ethics. But, according to what
principle does he deny them validity? If validity applies always
with respect to a standpoint and the world it envisions, then
Tillich's dismissal of other normative standpoints must be made
either dogmatically from his own standpoint or from a standpoint
that genuinely is beyond all other normative standpoints, a standpoint that comprehends them all. This is the standpoint of the
theology of culture. But, as we are about to see, the theology of
culture, whose standpoint Tillich takes throughout this address, is
heir to the intention of theological ethics, although it is not itself
essentially an ethical standpoint but a religious one. In summary,
Tillich's argument is that theological ethics cannot without contradiction maintain its claim to be a normative science, yet its
normative intention is not for this reason invalid—but then this
can be said of any normative-cultural standpoint just because, by
definition, it is one among many and it envisions a world. The
theology of culture is not supposed to be in danger of such a
defeat. It is not in danger of defeat because it will carry out the
valid intention of theological ethics not as ethics but as the science of religion.

Theology is the normative science of religion. Its correlate in
science is philosophy of religion. Theology so conceived is not, or
does not yet appear to be, the theology of culture. Nor does there
seem any reason why the normative science of religion should be
given the sole right to inherit the intention or goal formerly envisioned and pursued by theological ethics. That right seems properly to belong to ethics, philosophical and normative. Together
they decide upon the principles of justice by which human in-

stitutions must abide and upon the nature of the good so far as it is consistent with these principles. Tillich chooses not to meet this objection head on but to avoid its thrust and, speaking strategically, to turn its flank. I think that his strategy fails and will attempt to justify my belief in the exposition that follows.

Briefly, this is Tillich's strategy. As we have seen, he raises religion to a higher level than that occupied by other cultural domains. Its sovereignty extends over these domains, and because it is a higher sovereignty fundamental to the sovereignty of these others, it does not interfere with them and cannot be in conflict with them. But, this seems to be contrary to fact. Historically, religion is just another sphere of human culture whose bearers are religious societies, variously constituted. These societies, with varying degrees of exclusivity and tolerance, call themselves the church. And, there is ample evidence, past and present, of the church's interference in science, morality, art, politics, and so forth. This objection, however, is based upon a confusion. We must distinguish between the religious principle and historical religious reality, between religion as potency and religion as act. Only the former has the right of sovereignty not the latter. When this sovereignty is claimed in behalf of some historical religious institution, we have heteronomy, a violation of the rights of other cultural domains. When it is claimed consistently with the demands of the religious principle, the result is theonomy. Theonomy does not violate the autonomy of ethics or of any other cultural domain, rather theonomy fulfills autonomy and prohibits heteronomy.

How does Tillich justify this extraordinary role of the religious principle? All cultural realities, religion among them, have their origin in the human soul, in its spiritual or mental part. It has been customary to assign the different psychic activities that are productive of culture to different faculties of the soul, most commonly to three: a theoretical faculty, a practical faculty, and a faculty of judgment. From these originate the three basic psychic activities of knowing or representing, willing, and feeling,[40] and these in turn are the ruling functions, respectively, of science, ethics, and aesthetics: the three primary domains of human culture.[41] Tillich generally adheres to this construction of the mind, although, as we shall see, he wants to revise it. Religion, that is, the actuality of religion, differs from spheres of cultural life because its origin cannot be traced to a particular faculty. It seems obvious that representing originates from the theoretical faculty, choosing, from the faculty of the will, and being afraid or sad or gratified or some other feeling, from the feeling faculty. Thus, every attempt to relate religion to one of the psychic faculties is mistaken from the start. We, therefore, can dismiss the theories of religion put forward by Hegel, who relates it to the theoretical faculty, by Kant, who relates it to the practical faculty, and by Schleiermacher, who relates it to the feeling faculty. Only Schleiermacher has come close to the truth, because his theory "expresses the indifference of what is authentically religious towards its cultural expressions." Tillich does not explain how Schleiermacher's theory does this, but we may conjecture that it has something to do with the observation that follows concerning the presence of feeling in every cultural experience. If feeling is everywhere, then, like the religious potency, it is not essentially related in a special way to the other psychic functions or to their realizations. But, of course, feeling as such or in general is not inherently religious. If it were, then every psychic activity that involves feeling would be religious. But, this does not exclude the possibility that religion originates in a certain kind of feeling. Tillich considers this possibility and argues that if religion is assigned to some specific feeling, for example, a feeling of dependence, we could just as well argue that religion originates in the theoretical or the practical faculty. For, any special feeling, like the feeling of dependence, involves certain beliefs and certain actions as well as a certain kind of feeling. On Schleiermacher's behalf, one could respond that although this is true, it is clear that here feeling predominates and that Tillich's refutation founders on a confusion of psychic faculties with psychic acts. For example, choosing always involves some knowledge and some feeling, yet there is no uncertainty that it originates from the will. The same could be said about the feeling of dependence. About every psychic act, it can be said: "it is an activity of spirit in which something practical, something theoretical, and something emotional are joined together into a complex unity." But even if it were true that, in every complex psychic act, it is not possible to decide whether it is primarily representing, feeling, or willing, there is no need to trace the origin of the act beyond the soul and its faculties. What need is there for a religious potency, a potency that is beneath and above the other psychic potencies?

But, this is to digress, and at this point we must consider another digression that Tillich enters upon. In a modest and tentative way, he suggests a revision of the psychic organization. Instead of three faculties, it may be better to posit only two: the theoretical and the practical. The former is rather confusedly described. By means of this faculty, the mind is said to take its object into itself (the metaphor of knowledge as grasping and receiving) or theorizes, that is, intuits or looks directly at its object (the metaphor of knowledge as seeing). Here, the feeling faculty is called the aesthetic faculty or function and it is joined to knowing because both are theoria. Is the aesthetic function supposed to include all of feeling, and if not, if it only accounts for feeling of taste, how do we account for all the other feelings? By means of the second, practical faculty, the mind is said to try to enter its object "in order to shape it to suit itself." It is difficult to be sure what Tillich means by this metaphor or even to be sure what kind of a metaphor it is. But, if we consider Tillich's examples, society and law, it could be said that in fashioning conventions and laws to shape civil society, we are working from within, making a place for ourselves and our fellows. And, if we extend it to apply to technology or art, we often speak of entering into one's work. What is to be gained by this revision? There is economy, two faculties and two classes of functions instead of three, but at the cost of greater complexity and vagueness. So long as one wants to keep to a construction of the mind according to faculties and functions, the tripartite scheme seems the better one.[42] But, this is not our concern. Why does Tillich offer this revision here? Is it just an aside, a passing remark on how he regards this construction? Or, is there some other purpose, perhaps unacknowledged even to himself? For, as I have observed, it is unclear, in Tillich's construction, what happens to feeling. One suspects that feeling has been removed so that its place may be taken by religious potency.

This brings us to the next stage of Tillich's argument. We must distinguish between the religious potency and the religious act; that is, between the religious faculty and the religious function. The religious potency is defined as "a certain quality of consciousness." What is this quality? It is not what we are conscious of nor what we want or deliberately choose to do. Is it not a mood or a feeling? To be sure, not feeling in general but a certain kind of feeling. My guess, and it is only a guess but I trust not one frivolously made, is that Tillich proposes a revision of the psychic organization as part of an attempt to distance himself from Schleiermacher while at the same time appropriating his basic insight about the nature of religion as grounded in a certain kind of feeling. Why should he have wanted to distance himself from Schleiermacher? I do not know, but his reasons, whatever they might have been, are immaterial to our main concern, which is an exposition of his concept of religion.

If religion does not originate in one of the psychic faculties, or at least not in one that is on the same level with the theoretical and practical faculties, and if it is not a human response to an inference about the world and our place in it—Tillich does not consider this possibility at all—then where does it come from? Tillich's answer is that every religious reality is a complex production that originates in a religious principle, whose quality is transmitted to and carried by "an autonomous theoretical or practical" cultural reality. Basic to every religious reality is a duality. As a human actuality, realized by means of the faculties of the mind, it is autonomous, which is to say, it is an original human creation. But, as a religious reality, it also possesses the quality of religious potency, which it expresses. As such, it is not merely an original human creation but something more or, more precisely, a vehicle for something more. It is what Tillich will later call 'a symbol' for the religious potency.

A "specifically religious sphere" of culture arises, then, when cultural acts are joined to the religious potency or principle[43] that is discernible, a felt quality, only in this union. If we were to inquire who is the agent of this union, the answer is clear; it is not the human agent, nor would Tillich want us to think about an agent in this instance but, perhaps, about an agency, for example, the agency of grace. The products of this union are identifiably religious-cultural entities: myths, dogmas, religious standards of taste, types of religious personality, religious virtues, laws, moral rules, types of religious society. These are the specific forms of religion as a cultural reality. Yet, they are not the single domain of the religious potency. It cannot be contained by them nor could a consciousness in which this potency were active, for example, the consciousness of the theologian, be contained by them, because it is an absolute power. It would break through the sacred precincts and escape into the world.

Tillich then asserts, emphatically, that religion is actual in every cultural domain, by which I take him to mean that every cultural act expresses the religious potency. Thus, the actuality of religion pervades the whole of human culture. How this religious actuality is perceived in what is prima facie secular cultural reality is not explained here, nor is it clear how religion and secular culture come to be distinguished historically, if each expresses the same religious principle. In any case, the assertion that the religious potency is actualized everywhere in human cultural reality is supposed to account for the historical conflicts between religious and secular culture: since each may claim the absoluteness of the religious principle that each expresses, neither can tolerate the claim of the other. Yet, Tillich continues, there are no conflicts. Where, as has been the case in the past, specific religious cultural institutions dominate completely human cultural life so that the autonomous spirit cannot or does not know enough of itself to assert itself, there can be no conflict. A perfect heteronomy is not experienced as heteronomous. The modern age was marked by such conflicts, which continue today, but once the autonomous mind came to know its own powers sufficiently to assert itself, the conflict was won. Yet, there remains a division between religious and secular culture and, hence, a divided consciousness, which is intolerable and which will destroy consciousness. What is threatened is autonomy itself, the ability of the human soul to govern itself, through its faculties, according to laws it devises for itself, universally and in harmony with all other rational beings. The effect of this destruction would be a kind of cultural madness, a panic of the spirit, a free-for-all instead of a creative anarchy in which anything goes, a cultural war of all against all. One cannot overestimate the intensity of Tillich's insistence that the duality of religion and secular culture must be overcome.

The role of the theologian of culture becomes clearer. Aware of the religious principle that rules his consciousness, he cannot remain within the limits of an older religious culture that history has passed by, and under the banner of the religious principle, he enters the secular world as a champion of the autonomy of culture and of its religious substance.

The concept of autonomy will be an almost constant concern throughout the remainder of this essay, so I shall attempt briefly to characterize it here. Autonomy is the principle of secular culture. It is a principle of self-origination, self-motivation, and self-government applied to all human cultural activity. The activities of the mind that produce culture are spontaneous and self-originating, they follow rules that are their own invention, rules that are universal and shared without conflict by all human agents. These activities are not only self-determining but also self-appraising, and their productions can be shared by all, admired, appropriated without violence and willfull selfishness. These productions, properly understood, are the emblems of a form of life that is open and free. Heteronomy, on the other hand, is the subjection of the autonomous spirit to an alien law. Now, the theologian's standard and principal weapon is the religious potency, whose theonomous power is not supposed to violate autonomy but protect it and, perhaps, even enhance it.

How this is possible is to be made clear by a closer look at what religion is. Religious potency has been defined as a certain quality of consciousness joined to certain cultural acts that together compose a special sphere of religion. However, this union is not peculiar to manifestly religious things, because every cultural actuality expresses the religious potency. Therefore, the claim of a special sphere of religion is broken in principle.

In the last two paragraphs of this section, Tillich draws the same conclusion but in a somewhat different way. Here, religion is said to be a basic experience. Whether this is the same as "a certain quality of consciousness," is not clear. Unless a mood or a feeling conveys a certain metaphysical content, the answer would seem to be No. Religion is defined as the "experience of the unconditioned." It is a dual experience: "the experience of absolute reality on the basis of the experience of absolute nothingness." In the order of experience, absolute nothingness comes first. It, in turn, may—but Tillich does not say that it must—be preceded by various negative experiences: the impermanence and contingency of things, the decay of values, personal failure and the loss of identity, and the prospect of inevitable death. Absolute nothingness is interpreted as the absolute (unqualified) denial, pure and simple, of everything. Yet, it is not merely a logical act that is meant here. Its mood is more like a judgment or condemnation or a counsel of despair. However, when we reach this awareness of absolute nothingness, the value of this experience is completely transformed. Instead of unqualified denial of everything, everything is unqualifiedly affirmed. In each case, what is affirmed and denied is the same, namely, this totality of things, this world. Yet, something more than this world denied and affirmed is experienced, although we are cautioned against imagining it as a new or higher reality beyond the present reality that is given to experience. In this basic experience, a "reality forces itself upon us"; it comes upon us suddenly, no doubt mysteriously; it overwhelms us, as seems fitting for a religious reality. The best way to define it is negatively: "It is not a being, it is not substance, it is not the totality of beings." The mystical, neo-Platonic "what is beyond being" is a more fitting definition. It is both nothing and something, which is to say it cannot be adequately represented by any of our categories, which apply properly only to the experience of finite things. Yet, the limits of our understanding offer us no other way to represent it to ourselves. Perhaps, to invoke a mood of metaphysical perplexity, Tillich mentions the ancient confusion between the copula and the Existential 'is.' Saying that this reality 'is' anything hides what we are talking about: we are concerned not about an actual entity "but an actuality of meaning," and not just any meaning, but "the ultimate and most profound meaning." What does Tillich mean by the expression 'actuality of meaning' (*Sinnwirklichkeit*)? And how are we to interpret his further remark that it "convulses everything and builds everything anew." Clearly, 'everything' here does not mean just everything, but everything insofar as it has meaning for us. When this reality of meaning forces itself upon us, it completely shakes up the interpretation that we have given to our world. Perhaps it can be likened to the experience of reading a mysterious tale that captures our attention and holds it to the very end. When the ending comes, it takes us completely by surprise. In a moment of disclosure or revelation, all of our preliminary interpretations and expectations are overturned, everything that we have noted and arranged in our consciousness is brought to disorder, and as it were, the point of the story is presented to us as something new and unexpected and wonderfully satisfying. The actuality of meaning, then, is not just a plausible meaning of the whole of life, not even a goal that we may pursue with the greatest passion and abandon. It is the discovery of meaning that actually fulfills.

If this interpretation of Tillich's concept of an ultimate actuality of meaning is correct, then I do not see how it can be identified with the religious potency, for the religious potency is a potency and not an actuality and its realization is always in the form of some autonomous cultural act, which is not that potency but merely expresses it. Strictly speaking, its presence is discernible not as some meaning but as a quality of awareness of that meaning. Yet, there are religious meanings. It is not hard to think of one. Any apocalypse will do. Even so, perhaps what Tillich means by the ultimate actuality of meaning has to do not with the meaning itself, its content, but how it enters our consciousness, as though coming from beyond, overwhelming, surprising, fulfilling; in short, how it is experienced. On this interpretation, it doesn't really matter what the meaning is, or whether there is only one ultimate meaning for everyone, or where it really comes from. All that matters is the quality of awareness that marks religious reflection upon it. Yet, we shall see in the succeeding sections that these other things matter very much.

If religion is an experience of the disclosure of an ultimate meaning, which comes upon us suddenly and almost in one moment denies all the preliminary meanings we might have entertained and which, almost in the very same moment, affirms them all in a new way, like an artist who transfigures the commonplace and the ordinary, and if this denial and affirmation applies to everything that has meaning for us, to our world, then everything is taken up into the sphere of religion, so that there can be no conflict between religion and secular culture. But, how does this preserve the autonomy of culture? If the whole realm of science is denied and affirmed in the experience of ultimate meaning, and if thereby it becomes religious, then it is correct to conclude that there no longer is any justification for a special sphere of religious science. If all science is religious, then the fact that some science is religious does not make whatever the 'some' may denote especially religious; although Tillich allows that it is still possible, even necessary, to speak in a qualified sense of "special spheres of religious culture." But, the effect of the ultimate affirmation of all of science may not be to preserve the autonomy of science. This affirmation does not leave what is affirmed unchanged. Science is given a new interpretation, a theonomous one, and while it is no doubt true that cultural acts and things can be interpreted without being deprived of their autonomy, this may not be true of every interpretation. This will require a deeper inquiry into theonomy and its relation to autonomy, which brings us to the subject of the next section. However, before leaving this one, some leftover difficulties require our attention.

First, I am unconvinced that the "ultimate actuality of meaning" is necessarily religious. If it is not, then Tillich's definition of religion is not without more qualification a definition of religion. It all depends upon how one interprets the No and the Yes. I can think of two possible interpretations, one religious and the other not. I give the nonreligious one first. Call it high eroticism based upon nihilism. The affirmation of autonomy fits easily with an awareness of the groundlessness of one's interpreted world, the insubstantiality of one's existence, the impermanence of the whole of reality. Certainly, as early as *The Birth of Tragedy*, Nietzsche has presented a plausible view of how the highest human affirmation can be based upon the profoundest pessimism. There is no need to elaborate on it. Is this a religious view? Perhaps, but if it is religious, it is pagan, for its gods are gods of this world and, what is more, they are an autonomous human invention. At best, it is ironically religious. There is no doubt that it fits Tillich's definition of religion.[44] There is another interpretation, which is clearly religious. I have already suggested that the No might be interpreted as condemnation. Perhaps, the Yes can be interpreted correspondingly as forgiveness or as unqualified favor or grace. The autonomy denied is the old law, the law of sin; the autonomy preserved is the new law, the law of the new being in Christ. This also fits Tillich's definition and it is beyond doubt religious. Moreover, it is clear that Tillich intended an interpretation of the No and the Yes along these lines. I also believe that he did not intend this exclusively but rather intended a convergence of this interpretation and the one that I presented just before it along with others, for example, a neo-Platonic myth of the fall and the ascent of the soul. Yet, I also believe that he intended the scenario of justification to be the dominant interpretation. If my interpretation is correct thus far, and if the religious potency is just this scenario, then, the distinction between religious potency and religious act that is so important for the protection of autonomy and for the conquest of the conflict between religion and culture seems to be a specious distinction. Religion is not a quality of consciousness, it is a definite reflection about the meaning of life and the feeling that it evokes.

There are still other difficulties, and these I shall present as a set of contradictions and paradoxes that seem to follow from Tillich's theory of the relation of religion and culture.

    I. A. Every cultural reality is religious.
       B. Some cultural realities are not religious.
    II. A. A conflict between religion and secular culture is not possible.
       B. Conflicts between religion and secular culture have occurred.
    III. A. It is always the case that theonomy actualized is heteronomous.
    IV. A. A divided consciousness is universally repugnant.
       B. It is best for theology that the theologian have a divided consciousness.
       C. QED: What is best for theology is universally repugnant.

The first is a contradiction pure and simple. The first proposition is my interpretation of Tillich's claim that religion is actual in
every cultural domain, and it may be avoided by a different interpretation. Tillich's claim could be taken to mean that in every
cultural domain there are some specifically religious cultural realities. On this interpretation, the contradiction is dissolved. But,
clearly, this is not the right interpretation, for Tillich wants to
draw from this claim the conclusion that there is no separate
sphere of religious-cultural reality, neither in general nor in particular; that is, there is no religious science or ethics or aesthetics.
Again, on Tillich's behalf, it may be argued that Proposition A
attributes a religious quality to every cultural reality only in principle, or more precisely, it asserts that every cultural reality at
least is potentially religious. This certainly fits Tillich's thinking
about religion. Then, it could be said that the religious potency is
present everywhere as potency but like grace it is actual only
where it chooses to be, or it could be said that it is actual everywhere as the No but only somewhere, wherever it chooses, as the
Yes. But, this interpretation does not overcome the division between religious and secular culture and their conflicting claims
about science, morality, and taste. Moreover, Tillich does not say
that religion is potentially present in every cultural domain but
that it is actual. Perhaps, he is not making an assertion about how
cultural realities are but about how they ought to be or ought to
be interpreted. This, I think, offers the best prospect for escaping
the contradiction, but it is not certain whether in escaping we will
have to leave too much behind, nor is it clear that such a demand
is justified. One can deny the second proposition by claiming that
it is only apparently true. How so? If the religious potency is
actual in every cultural reality, then it must be discernibly present. What are we to look for? If Tillich were to respond that it is
present as the awareness of the nothingness that underlies all
cultural experience and as the courage nevertheless to persist in
cultural creation, one may challenge the right to interpret nihilism and this courage as fundamentally religious.

The second set of propositions also constitutes a contradiction, for what is not possible cannot occur. Conflicts occur when
the parties of the conflict take their stand on principles that they

believe to be incompatible. If the parties are rational, the conflict between them should end when they are shown that their respective principles are not incompatible. Then, with respect to these principles, it is true that there can be no conflict. The contradiction is dissolved if it can be shown that the conflicts between religion and culture, which have occurred and continue to occur, are based upon a misunderstanding of principles. Has Tillich shown this? So he has claimed. He has based his claim upon the distinction between religious potency and religious act. But, at the most, all that he is able to show is that religion and secular culture are not potentially in conflict, but that, actually, conflicts have occurred between cultural realities in which the religious potency is present in a way that is discernibly religious and cultural realities in which the religious potency is actual but incognito. This is not a very satisfying solution.

I shall leave III and IV for later consideration, for their interpretation depends upon discussions still to take place. These are not contradictions but only paradoxes, which in the last analysis may be permitted to stand.

3

In this third section of his address, Tillich will characterize the theology of culture according to its task, method, and divisions. To accomplish this, however, it is first necessary for him to clarify the concepts of autonomy, theonomy, and heteronomy, for theology of culture is a theonomous science. Its task is to explain the possibility of a theonomous cultural reality, to develop a philosophy of the history of culture from the standpoint of theonomy, to envision a system of the whole of culture from the standpoint of the theonomous principle. Whether he functions as a critic, philosophical historian, or visionary, whether he analyzes cultural things, typifies them, or projects an ideal system comprehending them all, the theologian uses the same hermeneutical principles: the categories of form, content, and substance. But, the latter principle is the principle or category of theonomy that in every case determines his point of view. Because theonomy is the correlate of autonomy and heteronomy is a false or counterfeit theonomy, an inquiry into the meaning of theonomy involves us in a consideration of the meaning of autonomy and heteronomy as well. Tillich, however, is concerned here only with autonomy and theonomy.

His definition of these terms is not very helpful. We are told, initially, not what autonomy and theonomy are, but how they are established or founded. Nevertheless, from what follows, it seems clear that theonomy and autonomy are standpoints or types of standpoint. Autonomy is a cultural-scientific standpoint founded upon the principle of form. Form here denotes the laws that govern the exercise of the cultural, that is, psychic, faculties or their functions: representing, willing, and feeling. Theonomy is a cultural-scientific standpoint founded upon the principle of substance, which is the reality that these laws or, more precisely, the rule-governed psychic activities represent or convey through their various cultural acts. This, I believe, is a fair account of what Tillich intends in the first two sentences of this section.

But why does he use the terms theonomy and autonomy to denote these standpoints? Perhaps a closer look at their meaning will help to answer this question. To get a better understanding of the meaning of the term 'autonomy', it is useful to go back to Kant, for there is no doubt that Tillich's use of the term, and, perhaps, of its fellows, is historically dependent upon Kant. Kant used the term to define a certain kind of causality, namely, the causality that resides in every rational being. He distinguishes autonomy from heteronomy, which is best represented as efficient causality, the causality of mechanical processes. Here, too, there are laws, and a rational account of them can be given. But the things that are determined by these laws are not self-determining, they have not, as it were, written or enacted these laws for themselves; they are not themselves the source of these laws. Although, it may be said that they obey reason, they are not rational beings, and their obedience, if they are conscious beings, is merely a matter of conditioning and not of free choice. Although reason generally is autonomous, Kant's main concern is with practical reason, with reason so far as it is the cause—and Kant's supposes an original causality here—of actions that have moral value. Morality is possible only if there are autonomous beings. Heteronomy also governs human actions. For example, whenever our actions are motivated by hunger or fear or desire, by our likes and dislikes, or when we are somehow compelled to act by another, then the causal process, whether physical or psychological, is no different from natural causality generally. And, there is nothing wrong with such motives, just as long as we do not allow them to overrule or replace our moral duty, which we determine autonomously for ourselves. Even self-interest is a heteronomous cause, for the self that is interested in its welfare, for example, in its safety, material wealth, reputation, or even in its eternal salvation, is not rationally self-determined when it gives in to these motives, rather it is subject to one emotion or another, to fear, envy, desire, vanity, the fear of death. The only feelings that are consistent with morality are those disinterested feelings that are involved in judgments of taste concerning the beautiful and the sublime. Tillich has broadened the scope of autonomy, not improperly and not without Kant's precedent, to apply to all human actions that originate in freedom. His version of the concept is a romanticized one that seeks universality in the original productions of genius rather than in the universal legislative power of reason. Another reason, perhaps, for disquiet. His concept of heteronomy seems to me to be different from Kant's, and although they are not incompatible and have points in common, there is no need to relate Tillich's concept to Kant's, except, perhaps, to observe that for both, heteronomy always is the source of false principles, whenever it is given sway over human activities that are supposed to originate in freedom. Kant, not surprisingly, has no concept of theonomy. But, at least in one important way, it relates very much to Kant. Tillich regards it as a corrective to Kantian formalism. But, this is an issue that we must take up later.

Autonomy and theonomy denote standpoints, but, as may be recalled from the first chapter, standpoints that belong to any cultural science are themselves cultural creations. They are creative viewpoints that take in the cultural creations within a particular sphere of culture or universality. Autonomy and theonomy represent universal standpoints. They take in the whole of culture. Is, then, the scientific work that proceeds from these standpoints creation? I think that the answer to this question must be Yes, if consistency is to be maintained. For taking a standpoint and doing scientific work from that standpoint are not different acts. Practically speaking, there is an analogy to virtue: just as one acquires virtue, as Aristotle observed, by acting virtuously, so one acquires a standpoint by doing creative things that reflect that standpoint, by working it out. But, with respect to theonomous standpoints, Tillich is hesitant to admit this, as we shall soon see. However, for him, the question is not whether the theologian of culture, whose standpoint is theonomous and who is imbued with theonomous power, is able to create—the answer to this question is undoubtedly Yes—but whether he should give way to the creative power and motivation within him. With respect to autonomous standpoints, Tillich attributes to them and to their works the status of creation, but he does not do so unequivocally, as I shall argue later. Indeed, on the interpretation of the concepts of theonomy and autonomy to follow, the more autonomous a standpoint, the less creative we would expect its work to be. An extreme of autonomy might display virtuosity and wit but not creativity. These are issues, however, whose time in this interpretation is still to come.

Autonomous standpoints, then, are concerned with form, that is, with the laws of cultural creation, laws laid down by the self-determined cultural creator. Theonomous standpoints have regard to the same laws, which is to say they respect the prerogatives of autonomy, but their concern with these laws and the things produced according to them is with their expressiveness. Not these laws as such but the reality, the spiritual substance, conveyed through them is what concerns theonomy. This leads to the rather curious conclusions that autonomous science and autonomous cultural creation are essentially indifferent to expression. Theonomy, on the other hand, does not legislate.

Having defined autonomy and theonomy, Tillich proceeds to lay down a law concerning their formations. "The more form, the more autonomy; the more substance, the more theonomy." This law, I take it, applies to all cultural creation, including the formation of standpoints. The more cultural creation conforms to its own laws, the more autonomous it is. The more expressive it is or the more spiritual substance it conveys or the more meaningful it is, then, the more theonomous it is. These seem to be tautologies. However, we may ask, is it also the case that the more autonomy the less theonomy and conversely the more theonomy the less autonomy? I am not sure that Tillich intends this, but I think that the way he develops this law and uses it, especially to attack formalism, implies it. Consider the image of the line Tillich employs to depict the relation between form and substance. Pure form and pure substance represent the extremities of the line. Between the extremes, which are absolute limits that are never realized, form and substance unite. With the aid of this image, are we supposed to imagine these combinations as various degrees of impurity? That is one interpretation but probably not altogether the correct one, because form and substance are meant for each other, they belong together. If we read further, to Tillich's account of the types of cultural formation (the second philosophical-historical division of the theology of culture), we find him once more making use of the culture line. We may read it as his gloss. Since form and substance belong together, we might expect that there is an optimum combination of both. Midpoint between the extremes of the culture line, form and substance unite in perfect harmony and equilibrium in a cultural creation that is the type of the classic.[45] But, if this is an ideal for Tillich—and I don't believe that it is[46]—it is nevertheless, a form of cultural realization not easily realized or maintained, for the marriage of form and substance, even if it were made in heaven, is a stormy one, filled with only occasional and illusory moments of harmony and tranquillity. On either side of the midpoint, then, form and substance tend to exclude each other from their cultural creations, although, Tillich is insistent that this exclusion can never be complete. Where autonomy predominates, there is a tendency towards the secular and the profane and, it follows from Tillich's scheme, a loss of expressivity, rather, to be precise, a loss of adequacy to express the reality, that is, the spiritual substance, "that it is supposed to contain." If the extreme of a pure autonomy can be characterized as "self-sufficient finitude," to borrow one of Tillich's later expressions, one must hasten to add that this sense of sufficiency must be an illusion. The inadequacy of form grows greater until it can no longer contain the spiritual substance, the pressure is overwhelming, the vessels of form are shattered, and spiritual substance is revealed in power. This overwhelming and shattering, Tillich adds are, nevertheless and paradoxically, themselves form. I am not sure what to make of this metaphor. Tillich more often uses another metaphor to depict the failure of autonomous formations to be meaningful, the metaphor of emptying, which I take to depict a process like abstraction, a preoccupation with pure design and an indifference towards concreteness. On this depiction, the loss of meaning or spiritual substance is deliberate, forms are not shattered but deliberately emptied by autonomous, rationally designing choice. This cultural result, then, is cause of a reaction from the other side of the culture line. But, the metaphor of the shattered vessels seems to mean something different. The cultural process that Tillich seems to be representing here, then, is not the deliberate emptying of form (which is a intellectual act—see his remarks on neo-Kantianism in Section 4 of the text and in Chapter 4 here) but the cheapening and depreciation of meaning. He is thinking of the commercialized cultural creation of the petit bourgeoisie rather than the will to purity of Enlightenment thinkers. How are we to interpret the paradoxical form by which substance is revealed? Is it theonomous or is it heteronomous? Is it a form deliberately devised, through some art, or is it merely the form that substance itself takes without thought or without art, in a moment of ecstasy or inspiration, like speaking in tongues? There are forms on the substance side of the culture line; if there were not then there could be no theonomous cultural creation. Of these two possibilities, is either heteronomous, or are both theonomous? How do we tell? Tillich says that it would be "the worst kind of heteronomy" to attempt to grasp substance apart from form, but according to his terminology, this grasping would not be a formative act, that is, not an act of shaping reality, but an attempt at cognition, a pure intuition of substance. This is a curious claim for someone whose entire religious epistemology is built upon the notion of the ultimate identity of the subjective and the objective and of ecstatic intuition.[47] If this is the extreme, what are the less extreme forms of heteronomy supposed to be like? In general, throughout his address, Tillich associates heteronomy most often with the formation of a special realm of religious culture alongside autonomous secular culture and in conflict with it for the right to control various cultural domains. Even a religious culture that succeeds in gaining universal dominion and suppresses every challenge of autonomy and thereby prevents conflict is heteronomous.[48] For the same reason, he hesitates and vacillates about the creative role of the theologian of culture, who is not allowed to enter into the act of creating a theonomous or religious system of culture, who can only envision it. Does this mean that every actual cultural formation that occurs on the substance side of the culture line is heteronomous? If it does, then the answer to the question previously put is that the paradoxical forms said to reveal substance, however fashioned, are heteronomous. I do not believe that this is what Tillich intends, but I do not see how he can avoid coming to this conclusion. And, if I am correct, then Tillich's theology of culture is self-defeating.

But, let us for now, keeping to Tillich's intentions, look once more at his system of cultural formation. He believes that there is a clear conceptual distinction between autonomy and theonomy and between theonomy and heteronomy, and that formally or theoretically, autonomy and theonomy constitute different polar types of the union of form and substance in a cultural creation, and that heteronomy is a false theonomy. And, let us further recall that form and substance, the principles of autonomy and theonomy, are meant for each other, just as autonomy and theonomy as standpoints look to each other as correlates, and that the perfect union of these two elements is a well-formed cultural creation in which neither predominates, the classic. But, let us also not forget that the classic is not the place where the theologian of culture takes his stand. With this in mind, let us proceed to an examination of the method, the divisions, and the aim of the theology of culture.

A brief review of the work of the theology of culture should make it clear why the theologian of culture avoids the classical standpoint. His responsibility is to the appearances of substance in concrete religious expression wherever they occur, and he takes his stand on the principle of substance in the conviction that these occur everywhere or, at least, wherever cultural creations manifest greatness, and for Tillich greatness is always to be associated with the disorder of creation, with the titanic and the awesome moment of tragic denouement, with the sublime and the dionysian.[49] This theological-cultural work, if it is scientific, cannot be done without a method. The theologian of culture employs a theological method that is yet to be defined. He applies this method not, as the church theologian, to ecclesiastical life or to dogma but to the whole of culture. Tillich justifies this universal use of a theological method by noting that he is just following a common procedure among the cultural sciences. If other cultural

scientists can present the whole of culture by means of a sociological or a psychological method, whether critically and re-
ductively or normatively and constructively Tillich does not say,
then surely, to sharpen his justification, the theologian can do the
same with his method. Methods have a home, but they are free to
travel. This seems to be a score for pluralism, but, does this not
make the threat of a divided consciousness even greater? Moreover, if theology of culture derives its method by abstraction from
a concrete theological standpoint, from the theology of the
church with all of its historical limitations—for a method consists
of categories and concepts of interpretation, which although abstract in form reflect some concrete experience—and if to be
useful any abstraction must be thought concretely, most properly,
concretely with respect to its historical moment of origin, can
heteronomy be avoided? And, if it could, how are we to distinguish between a heteronomous and a theonomous use of the
theological method? Perhaps, we can answer these questions
after we have had a closer look at the divisions of the theology of
culture and its method.

Like any normative-cultural science and like church theology in particular, a theology of culture originates with the
creation of a standpoint in three moments: there is a general
conceptual grounding, followed by a philosophical-historical
construction, and these two preliminary moments are taken up
by the theologian of culture, who, through a self-positing act,
shapes them into a concrete standpoint. The general concepts of a
theology of culture have already been introduced: form and substance, with content as a third, and the No and the Yes. These are
the elements of the theological method. The historical construction, as already noted, is a typology of "great historical creations"
of high culture, of sublime achievements, presented from the
point of view of "the religious substance realized in them"; that
is, not in terms of their formation but in terms of their expressive
power. Finally, the theologian must fashion "an ideal design for a
culture religiously fulfilled" that he carries out "from his own
religious standpoint." Tillich does not make clear the identity of
this special religious standpoint. Is it the concrete standpoint that
the theologian of culture held within the church before he was

driven out into the world in his quest for the unity of consciousness, or is it a new concrete standpoint, one that is free from
confessional encirclements? I think it is the former; the latter
cannot exist so long as the theologian of culture refuses to be a
creator. The theologian refuses to create because it is unlawful for
him to do so, for were he to create on the basis of his theonomous
ideal, he would commit heteronomy.

More about this interesting paradox will be forthcoming, but
before we come to it some other difficulties require our attention.
Tillich's threefold division of the theology of culture simply re-
duplicates the threefold division of any science of culture, and
this seems quite natural. His description of the task of the first
division as cultural analysis, "a general religious analysis of
culture," is what one would expect. What should correspond to a
normative-theonomous science of culture but a religious philosophy of culture. But theology of culture as such is a normative
science, in this case not the normative science of religion but the
normative science of the religious aspect of all of culture. What
kind of work does the religious philosophy of culture do? Analytical and critical. Does this involve the derivation of basic concepts
of the theological method? If we look more closely, we observe
that two pairs of concepts are employed in the religious analysis
of culture. The Yes and the No are derived from an analysis of
religion, from Tillich's brief sketch of a philosophy of religion.
Substance, form, and content are general categories derived from
an analysis of culture. We would expect that their derivation is
accomplished not by a religious philosophy of culture but by
philosophy of culture pure and simple. So, the religious analysis
of culture, which is the first division of the theology of culture, is
a composite of two cultural-philosophical disciplines, a union of
philosophy of religion and philosophy of culture. The justification
for this union follows from the concept of religion presented in
the previous section. According to this concept, religion is not just
another part of culture but the basis of culture as a whole. But, if
Tillich's concept of religion is the right one, then the philosophy
of religion and the philosophy of culture are one and the same.
And, this becomes more apparent when it is noted that substance
and the No and Yes are identical concepts. Substance is the abso-

lute reality of meaning, it is revealed in a shattering of form that is form, it denies and affirms form. But if the religious analysis of culture is the philosophy of culture, does this mean that a secular philosophy of culture is no longer needed, indeed, is no longer valid? "Not at all," Tillich would answer. For the religious analysis of culture is a philosophy of culture from the standpoint of substance, whereas a secular philosophy of culture is such from the standpoint of the autonomy of form. The answer has a deceiving clarity to it. What about the concept of substance? Who is responsible for its derivation, the religious analyst or the philosopher of culture? If the former, does it thereby become a valid concept for the latter? Why should the philosopher pay attention to this alien concept that appears to come from a ghostly double? If the latter, does he understand its import? Expression is not a strange term to secular critics and philosophers of culture, but perhaps they don't understand its deepest meaning.[50] But, this is to suggest that autonomy is an illusion, the term a mere slogan, for it would be constitutionally unable to accomplish the critical evaluative, much less the creative, work that it claims to do. Surely, if substance is an appropriate concept to represent what is expressed in painting or music or the novel, and so forth, then the secular philosopher ought to be able to derive it on his own. Paradoxical form is still form and, therefore, should not escape his purview. And, if this applies to what is expressed by form, it applies even more to meaning. But, suppose the secular philosopher derives this concept and finds it not to be religious, is he mistaken? On whose authority? The religious analyst? But why should the secular philosopher be bound by what the religious analyst says? Here, I suppose one may appeal to correlation. But that concept is too problematic to be able to settle anything just by making an appearance and, anyway, the proper correlate of a philosophical science is not another philosophical science but a normative systematics, although it could be a secular-normative systematics. It would seem, therefore, that we have two competing philosophies of culture, one religious and the other secular, or at least one that is not religious in Tillich's sense of the term. Does not the theologian of culture find himself in the same predicament that, as church theologian, he found so intolerable? And, if doubleness and divided consciousness is a mark of heteronomy, does not theonomous science turn out to be an agent of heteronomy? Let the theologian abandon all claim to form, even the paradoxical form of the manifestation of substance. Let him refuse even to speak or gesture in behalf of substance, but attend to it in silence. If silence is not a form, perhaps he will avoid heteronomy. The last proposition of Wittgenstein's *Tractatus* seems most expressive here: "Wovon man nicht sprechen kann, darueber muss man schweigen."[51]

In his discussion of the task of the first or analytical part of the theology of culture, Tillich introduces the concept of content. Content, we are told, is not the same as substance. It is the mere objectivity or factualness of sensuousness or naturalness of a cultural reality. For example, it is what a picture might be said to be 'of' or to depict, some ordinary thing or scene, even a figure or a face. Content is not what a picture expresses or means. Only when the factualness of the object is formed or transfigured through the artist's vision of it does it enter the sphere of culture. Of course, if it is an artifact, then it enters the cultural world twice.[52] But, in its second entry, it takes on artistic meaning, it becomes expressive. Of the three—form, substance, and content—content has the least value. However, it is also the bearer of substance, which form draws into it in order to bring substance to expression. Tillich says it is accidental. It is just there to be taken up into a creative act or left alone. But, surely, he cannot mean that once content is taken up into a creative configuration it continues to be accidental. If, by accidental, we mean the quality of dispensability, the quality of a thing whose presence or absence makes no difference, then the content of a well-formed cultural creation cannot be said to be accidental, even when, in certain cultural formations, a content may appear transitory, unsubstantial, ghostly, or as something that is there by chance. But, I think that this is what Tillich must mean. Form is said to play the role of mediator between substance and content. By means of form, substance is introduced into content that, as formed content, thereby becomes expressive; by the same mediation, substance becomes concrete. (Or is it form that becomes concrete? In which case, content may also be said to play the role of mediator.) In a well-formed figure, there can be no conflict between content and form. But, the harmony of a well-formed cultural reality may be disrupted by a sudden influx of substance. Is this disruption equivalent to a loss of autonomy? A shattered form is one that has lost its formative power or, at least, its containing power and, to that extent, its autonomy. Likewise, with the shattering of form, the content may appear ghostly, unnatural, or decomposed. It should be noted here that the form that is shattered, decomposed, denaturalized is not abstract form but the figure of the object as we expect it to be from everyday experience. Since religious substance, or substance interpreted religiously, causes this effect, the decomposition of the form of content amounts to a transition from autonomy to theonomy, from a secular to a religious condition. This transition, then, is not the work of art, but of something beyond art, beyond any merely human art of expression or representation. But, is such a transition from the secular to the religious necessary? Is secular sensibility inherently insensitive to moods of estrangement? Is secular sensibility able only to perceive a well-fitting relation between form and content; are ill-fittedness and distortion forms whose interpretation requires a theonomous, that is to say, a religious, point of view? Is the dark side of life revealed only to the religious thinker? Is the abyss something that opens up only to religious consciousness? To all of these questions, the right answer is No. To claim otherwise seems, in Tillich's own view, heteronomous.

But I must avoid being unfair to Tillich. For this reason and in order to avoid the charge that all this talk of form and content and substance and their neat relations and correlations is no more than a game played with concepts; that is, mere formalism or, what may be worse, mere wordplay. In order, therefore, to give substance to all this talk and to satisfy the need to think concretely, I offer a couple of examples.[53] The examples are both histories. In what follows, I shall try as much as possible to follow Tillich's method of "cultural-theological analysis" as a test of its methodological validity. A history is a cultural creation. Therefore, on Tillich's construction, it consists of form and content, or formed content, and a certain meaning that both pervades and transcends it. The historian is a creator, which, of course, does not contradict his claim to be a scientist. The historian's content is an aggregate of some kind. For example, a historian of philosophy, writing about Heraclitus, confronts a collection of fragments, sayings by the philosopher and testimonies about his life and thought. His task is to work them into a suitable form, to make form fit content. Historical form is narrative, in this case, the narrative of Heraclitus' thinking, which begins to take shape in the imagination of the historian when he views the theme somehow coming forth from the fragments themselves. A well-formed narrative fits the content in such a way that it is no longer a mere aggregate but a totality; one, however, that must be read, that takes time, even if, as in this instance, it be only the inner temporality of a mind thinking. What makes something a narrative is not a mere sequence but a construction, a plot, whose organizing principle is a moment of greatest self-awareness, which, like a standpoint, takes in the whole. Ideally, the plot should incorporate all of the fragments and should fit them perfectly, but more often, a selection must be made for the sake of the unity of the narrative. The historian is aware of this limitation. The unincorporated fragments, then, may be said to be a threat to the unity of form. They can enter the narrative only by interrupting it, although the narrative art does not lack ways of incorporating such interruptions. As such, however, they disrupt the unity of the narrative, they draw our attention away from the narrative and reflection upon them may, finally, shatter the form altogether. When this occurs, the narrative that was supposed to contain this content suffers a loss of validity. Its claim to fit the content has been defeated. Following Tillich's method, we should say that form has lost "its natural and necessary relation to content." Like a balloon that has lost its mooring, form becomes detached and free floating. It becomes an abstraction. But, in this condition it becomes powerfully expressive, for it stands in immediate relation to substance. It becomes form in the paradoxical sense. How can this be? I suppose that an abstraction is a paradoxical form in the sense that it is a form of nothing in particular, in the same way that being, the supreme abstraction, is paradoxically nothing in particular. Tillich says that form allows this to happen to itself, as though the will to abstraction were a will to become paradoxical form and thereby to occasion the revelation of substance, of the No that, of course, is then to be followed by the Yes. But, how does this apply to our example? Form has been shattered, not by substance, but by its content. The content, all of it, then leaves the form that was supposed to contain it and returns to its original form. It again becomes a collection of fragments, aphorisms. This, too, might be called paradoxical form but not because it is abstract. Keeping to our example, there seems to be no need to employ the concept of substance as theonomous pole in relation to form and content. And, therefore, there is no need to travel to the other side of the culture line. The meaning, what is supposed to be expressed by the narrative and its content, resides in and comes to us from the content. Heraclitus was a philosopher. His fragments are themselves meanings, the utterances of thought about the cosmos, being and becoming, the dissemblance of nature, the universality and rarity of thought, the ecstasy and the despair of the thinker, life and death. These meanings pervade and surround any history of Heraclitus. Neither the literary remains of Heraclitus nor the historical reconstruction of them fully contain this substance of thinking. Is this substance, the sum of the meanings of Heraclitus' fragments, religious? We know how Tillich would answer. Let us, for the moment, grant him this. It is religious. But then, these meanings are not some mysterious substance, but thoughts, some of them more or less expressive than others. The form in which they come to us, fragmentary utterances, randomly arranged, heightens their meaning. They lend themselves to Expressionist interpretations. But it should be clear that Tillich does not derive the revelation of religious substance from here, not from the content but from the self-emptying of form. But, why should form allow itself to be shattered by substance and emptied? How does this emptying or shattering relate to historical construction and interpretation? It depicts the pathos of any conscientious historian, whose dissatisfaction with his constructions is chronic, and who, if he is an idealist and a romantic, may be captivated by the thought of the nothing from which he believes all of his historical constructions come. But there is no need to reflect on the limitations of the historian in this way. Realism, together with a moderate skepticism and a touch of irony will do as well to console the historian, and this point of view will also contribute more to the work of autonomous cultural science than a view that seems to glorify the pathos of failure.

Let us take another brief example: a history of some important event in the past, a war. The content in this instance consists of the events as recorded and reported in various records and, beyond these, the human past itself. The form is the narrative that shapes the content from the historian's perspective, his thematic interests: he may be a military historian, or a political historian, and so forth. There may be broader moral themes that govern the shaping of his narrative: human folly, for example. Churchill's themes, which we are to reflect upon as we read his narrative of the second World War, quaintly illustrate the latter: in the first volume, "How the English-speaking peoples through their unwisdom, carelessness, and good nature allowed the wicked to rearm," and the last volume, "How the great democracies triumphed and so were able to resume the follies which had so nearly cost them their life."[54] The content of such a history far exceeds anything that the narrative may embrace, yet the form also includes more than the content. As Simmel observed, "the historian says more than he actually knows in the strict sense," for content, no matter how richly represented, is always fragmentary. The historian must fill in and embellish. But, he also "says less then he knows" for his research takes in much more than he is able to present and he selects from it only what is significant from his point of view. If more were to be admitted than what fits, then such intrusions might take the form of anecdote, that is, a timeless moment that interrupts the narrative. What is substance or meaning here? It is human life itself, that great and persistent, but not eternal, stream of folly and decay and disappointment and longing that comes from nowhere and rushes towards a great abyss, its origin unrecorded and its end ultimately to be forgotten. Therefore, does not every self-contained history appear finally as an anecdote, an interruption in the flow of time? Dark as we may make it, there is always light enough to discern some form. If substance is not an invention of the formative mind, it is at least a most adaptable instrument of expression, of religious expression as well as other kinds. Perhaps, it is by means of mood, especially irony, that form conquers substance. Thus, although the examples confirm the validity of three elements of meaning: form, content, and substance, there seems to be no need of a law of substance set apart. The spontaneous and original formative power of autonomy, conscious of its limitations, seems sufficient.

But, if this makes unnecessary the first division of the theology of culture, it should not be forgotten that there are still two more parts, and that of these two, the third and normative part is that critical for the entire construction.

The second task of the theology of culture is to fashion a typology of the forms of cultural life or of cultural creation and a philosophy of history. I have already touched upon this in connection with Tillich's construction of the culture line. The typology is developed a priori from the polar relation of the two basic elements of meaning, form and substance. Hence, it is a philosophical construction and belongs to the work of concept formation. By this method, three basic types are formed: one, which exhibits the predominance of form, is a secular type of historical-cultural reality; another, which exhibits the predominance of substance, is religious; a third, in which both elements are in equilibrium, is the classical type. These, as we have already seen, correspond to the three most identifiable and, hence, most decisive points along the line of culture: the two ends and the middle. However, because any line is infinitely divisible, there is plenty of room for "intermediate and transitional stages," and because this is a construction of history, we may suppose that historical time proceeds back and forth along the line in the guise of a sequence of tokens of types and subtypes. Why Tillich singles out "the variety of forms of concrete religion" as a special cause of the diversity of types is not clear to me. The explanation that comes most readily to mind is that this is because substance is the source of meaning in every cultural creation, and religious formations are especially expressive. The second historical task, one might expect, should be a normative one. It involves the construction of a philosophy of history that, employing the theory of historical types, relates the historical present systematically to the past. We might expect it to be normative because, from Tillich's earlier discussion of cultural science, it is supposed to involve a justification of a present normative standpoint. But, Tillich says nothing of this. The philosophy of history merely produces "a philosophical-historical classification." But, is this not just another round of typology? In any case, here, too, the work done can be done from the standpoint of autonomy. It is formative work, and unless we are to have a duality of forms, each competing for the same content, and a divided consciousness, there seems to be no need for a special theonomous philosophy of history.

We come now to the third and final division of the theology of culture. This should be the climax of Tillich's address. The conceptual and historical tasks are only preliminary to the constructive work of the theologian. Even if these preliminary tasks are the work of others, as may be appropriate, there still remains much work to be done within theology's proper domain. The theologian of culture is supposed to be doing his most characteristic work as a maker of norms. Yet, Tillich's initial observation casts doubt also on the propriety of the theologian doing just this work. Up until now, we have been led to believe that the theologian is supposed to be "a religious systematizer of culture," which is to say, all of his labors are supposed to culminate in a construction of the whole of culture, a vision or revision of the whole in terms of its ultimate theonomous meaning. Substance, like the idea of the good, will lend its light to bring about a transfiguration of the whole. Now, Tillich says that the theologian cannot do this; he cannot because by doing so, he would subvert the validity of his position. Were he to create a theonomous system of culture, the result would be heteronomous. And, because he cannot without defeating his purpose, he must not. There are only two possible standpoints from which to create any cultural reality, the standpoint of form or the standpoint of substance. For the theologian to create from the standpoint of form would be to commit trespass, to infringe upon another's right. But to do so from the standpoint of substance, pure substance, is impossible, for substance finds expression only through form.

Let us pause here for a moment. When Tillich states that the theologian has the option to create from the standpoint (or 'side'—reference is to the culture line), of form or of substance, one or the other not both and no more, does he mean a standpoint of pure form or of pure substance, or does he mean by 'side of form' and 'side of substance', a type of standpoint in which form or substance predominates? If he means the former, then he cannot be referring to any actual standpoint—because every actual form is expressive of substance, even if only in the smallest degree, and every actualization of substance is something formed, is conveyed by some formed content—and a standpoint, at the very least, is something actual. If he means the latter—and he surely must—then actualized substance of this standpoint is already unlawful, that is, heteronomous, by virtue of its actuality. Thus, it would appear that the theologian not only cannot create but he cannot even take an actual standpoint. We were told in Section 1, almost at the start, that taking a standpoint is a creative act. So it would appear that the theologian can have no standpoint at all, indeed, in reality, cannot be a theologian.

I turn to Tillich's solution to the theologian's dilemma. We all know that the theologian must fashion a standpoint, must create, we only need to find out how. Tillich's answer is that he creates but not directly. What does this mean? First of all, it means that the theologian does not try to be creative in any of the special domains of culture. He does not try to fashion a religious or theonomous science or morality, or jurisprudence or art—we shall inquire soon whether Tillich abides by this prohibition. This solution seems to miss the point. Of course, the theologian is neither a moral philosopher nor a normative ethicist, neither a philosopher of art nor an aesthetician, and so forth, for unlike them, his domain is the whole of culture, whereas theirs apparently is not. So, his influence within these domains is only indirect, but this is not the same as creating only indirectly. What he creates, an ideal of culture, he creates directly. Unless Tillich means that it is not possible to create and at the same time maintain a view of the whole of culture. Thus, further on, he says that the theologian "may point generally in the direction in which he perceives the fulfillment of a genuine religious cuture"; that is, he can point the way, "but he cannot himself create the system."

The reason that he gives for this conclusion is that the theologian, by attempting to create his system, would cease to be a theologian and become a critic, he would be caught up in the richness of cultural life and in the autonomous rules of criticism, whose 'sovereign power' would drive him in directions that are contrary to his intentions. It is as though the theologian who wants to create is in danger of being seduced by culture, by its creative anarchy, driven here and there by powerful forces that obey their own laws, laws that are alien to the purity of theonomous vision.

There may be another interpretation of the options available to the theologian when he undertakes his constructive task. This interpretation presents not what Tillich meant but what he might have meant. The theologian might have considered two options, one from the side of substance and the other from the side of form, both pure. This interpretation requires that we set aside Tillich's rule that pure standpoints are never actual. Yet, I think, it must be set aside if one is to escape the theologian's dilemma. According to the concept of a theology of culture as it has been developed by Tillich thus far, it would appear that a universal cultural science is possible only from the standpoint of substance, that autonomous sciences and autonomous creations are man-ifold and fragmented, rich and diverse. And, hence, to enter into the world of secular culture, with its rich and abundant life, is to abandon the only place from which a truly universal view of culture is possible. The two options, then, reduce to one: a stand-point of pure substance. There are historical antecedents for this: Parmenides vision of pure being and Spinoza's standpoint of eter-nity, so Tillich is in good company. We must not forget, however, Tillich's remark made at the end of the next to last paragraph of this section that the philosopher of culture may also contribute to the realization of the unity of culture "from the standpoint of pure forms," that is, by deriving a set of categories basic to all spheres of culture, categories of meaning such as form, content, and substance and, perhaps, also by justifying their universal employment. So, there is still a conflict of options. But the conflict perhaps can be dissolved if we take Tillich's remark as an after-thought, one that might be elaborated in the following way: of course, it is possible to establish a standpoint on the basis of pure form, but such a standpoint can never be concrete and from it nothing concrete can be fashioned unless the pure forms are applied to life which is beyond mere thought. When this occurs, then other faculties besides the theoretical faculty come into play and the mind directs itself outwardly towards the activities of a manifold and varied and changing life: experience and intuition enter in; the activities of mind and its products divide and fragment, become expressive in many and various ways; and unity is restored only by a difficult return to pure thought. A pure autonomous standpoint is reached only by reflecting upon the logical structure of the mind. It is the form of pure self-reflection, the negative limit of expressivity. This, as we shall see in the next chapter, is the ideal form of philosophy. But, I have digressed and must now pick up the thread of argument.

If the theologian of culture cannot directly create the system of culture, then just what does he do? As Tillich describes it, he assumes the stance of a critic, affirming and denying the autonomous productions of culture. On the negative side, he reproaches current culture for its failure to create adequate vehicles of expression. In addition, as we have seen, he points the way towards "the fulfillment of a genuine religious culture," but he avoids any further involvement in bringing this about. He is, in fact, a creator. He fashions his own standpoint; although contrary to his initial impulse to leave the church and enter the world, he remains aloof from worldly creation, "far from every restriction to a determinate sphere"; he occupies the standpoint of pure substance; like the demiurgos of Plato's *Timaeus*, he takes up the "material at hand," in this case the manifold and chaotic stuff of cultural life, and "sketches out a religious system of culture, separating and joining as directed by his theological principle," which is his guide. Is this principle pure substance, or is it a more concrete principle, a concrete norm, which the theologian takes from his former theological surroundings? The text provides no answer. Let us suppose that it is the former, substance, the pure power of expression, analogous, perhaps to Plato's idea of the Good. And the outline that the theologian makes, a sketch of a thoroughly unified culture and cultural powers, "a synthesis of the highest significance," is this outline an actual creation? No, it is only a program for others to observe. The theologian does not directly create. What is it then? It is the ideal of culture, envisioned by him. But, this is something created by him, to be sure not for its own sake but for the sake of substance, so that it may find an adequate means of expression everywhere. In the light of the principle of expression, the theological principle, the theologian fashions the ideal of culture, the model to which all creators of culture—be they scientists, artists, moralists, or critics—must look and from which they must take direction in their work. However, the theologian looks not only to his principle and to the matter at hand while he creates the ideal, he also looks out from his lonely place across the chaos of cultural life to the distant horizon where there appears another lonely figure, the philosopher, who envisions not the ideal but only the formal possibility of culture in general, only concepts. We should not forget, however, that among these concepts and supreme, is the concept of being itself, which, here and elsewhere in Tillich's work, is the theoretical basis of universality in theological discourse.[55]

Is this vision of a cultural cosmos that is unitary in its expression of religious meaning an actual cultural creation, or is it not? It is, even if only in outline, even if incomplete, and even if meant for others to act upon, an actual norm. So, it is actual. And as a norm, must it prescribe? How does it prescribe? Does it merely suggest by its ideal presence, or does it present itself with a sterner, more outspoken authority that demands its due? Even if the theologian creates no more than this outline of a normative vision, he expects others to act upon it. It is said that he reproaches. To what end? If the envisioning of a cultural ideal does no more than produce visions that are realized nowhere but in the imaginations of those who stand apart, then of what value are they? Are they meant merely to console? Even consolation is a genuine cultural creation. But, as Tillich's final paragraph shows, the theologian of culture speaks with a more urgent voice than the voice of consolation. His appeal is not for resignation but for action, for cultural synthesis, the nature of which only he under-stands. By claiming this, Tillich rules out other normative con-structions of a cultural ideal. So he has created something that is supposed to be theonomous. But theonomous intentions not-withstanding, is it heteronomous? Before answering, let us turn to the next section and observe the theologian at work.

4

In the fourth section of his address, Tillich offers us some examples of the theologian at work. These examples are not chosen randomly but together represent all the spheres of culture—art, science, and morality—that correspond, respectively, to the three faculties of the mind—the aesthetic, the cognitive, and the practical. He tells us, furthermore, that they are for the most part exemplary only of the first of the theologian's three tasks, that is, an analysis of culture in terms of the basic concepts of form, content, and substance. Only occasionally, he says, will he make reference to historical typology, but it is his intention to avoid the third task, for to undertake this task would require justification of his "concrete theological principle," that is, of his ideal. If challenged to justify embarking even on the first task, Tillich could argue in one of two ways. He could argue, as he did in the previous section, on the basis of a principle of common practice. On the basis of this principle, he could claim the right to employ a critical method that admittedly has its roots in theology—this would apply to the No and the Yes—for the universal use of a method derived from the study of a particular sphere of culture is common practice among the cultural sciences. Or, he could argue that the concepts he employs are not basically theological concepts but universal categories of meaning that can be derived by a purely critical method, such as the Kantian method of transcendental analysis. The two arguments are not incompatible. Common practice may be vaguely reflective of an underlying universal structure of the mind. However, Tillich's theological method, although it depends upon the categorial scheme of form, content, and substance, which he believed could be derived and justified philosophically, does not merely use these concepts but interprets them normatively. Denial and affirmation are not merely dialectical acts, they reflect, in Tillich's employment of them, a positive theological content and hence belong to the theologian's ideal and their justification depends upon the justification of the theologian's concrete standpoint. That justification depends upon the construction of a normative philosophy of history, which, on the basis of a typological analysis, would show that the theologian's concrete standpoint or ideal is the right one and the only right one for the time, that it alone is opportune. Lacking this justification, we must assume that the examples given in this section are without justification, without the very justification that would be required if Tillich were to give examples of the theologian carrying out the second and third tasks of his discipline.

There is another observation to be made in this preliminary discussion. A review of the examples shows that the kind of work that they exemplify is not the critical analytic work of concept derivation that belongs to the first task—and that, we have seen, belongs to the philosopher and not to the theologian—but is critical only in the sense of normative judgments about the expressive value of cultural realities. This work belongs not to the first task of the theology of culture as Tillich outlined it in the previous section but to the indirectly creative work that Tillich assigns to the third task of a theology of culture. Because of this, Tillich can say that traces of the system or ideal "shine through the analyses." This fits with the argument that I made in the previous chapter, that the proper work of a theology of culture belongs only to this third task.

In this fourth section, then, we are presented with examples of the indirectly creative work of the theologian of culture, who has already envisioned his ideal, his concrete theological principle, and who permits it to be reflected in normative judgments about the expressive value of cultural creations. Neither method nor ideal have been justified. I doubt that they can be justified, at least not in the way that Tillich supposed they could be and not with the authority that Tillich sought for them. But these are issues that have been reserved for the last chapter.

Before turning to the examples, I have some further remarks to make about the theologian's work. In Plato's *Timaeus*, the work of creation involves shaping matter. From his standpoint of detachment, the creator looks in two directions, toward the eternal archetype, "that which is and never becomes," and toward the material at hand, "that which is always becoming and never is."[56] However, according to Timaeus' account in the dialogue, matter is not utterly formless, it has its own forms which are discerned by the demiurge and employed in the execution of his design, so that the forms imposed upon matter are not altogether alien to it but are in some sense proper.[57] Thus the demiurge might be said to respect matter, so far as it displays some form, but this does not prevent him from fitting it to a higher form. The work of the theologian of culture may be said to be like this. We must assume that he has already taken his position above things, that his standpoint is already established and that he is looking from there toward the material at hand. The material at hand is the historical world, which is always becoming and never is (a fitting description), a world shaped according to its own multifarious laws, whose domains combine in a barely perceptible order that seems to emerge out of disorder but which itself is constantly changing in its aspect. These forms and this ordered disorder, when "separated and joined," to use Tillich's words so reminiscent of the *Timaeus*, seem able to reflect a higher order, one that is ideal, perfect, and unchanging. So that one might suppose that the material at hand is destined to become a visible god.

Unlike the demiurge, however, the theologian cannot claim for his ideal true eternity and perfection. The ideal, according to which he judges worldly things, is made up of forms that originate from the same stuff as the material whose refashioning he wants indirectly to bring about. In this respect, he is not unlike the secular critic, who also affirms and denies according to criteria that are immanent in the productions of culture, who draws out of these formed things criteria that seem fit to become norms and sublimates them, who also has visions of cultural totalities, and whose nay-saying may be as harsh as the theologian's when cultural realities fail to measure up to these ideals. The difference, if there is one, must be that the ideals of secular critics have only the substance and duration of fashion. If they are abundantly endowed with autonomous creative power, they may shine and fill the world like a momentary sun, but the theologian looks to the true sun, to pure spiritual substance, which he knows, thanks to the philosopher, is equivalent to and has the grounding power of being itself. On the other hand, it might be said that the ideals of some secular critics (and artists and moralists, etc.) are not mere fashions but have true expressive power, but this is because they are theologians without knowing it. The theologian of culture is on the lookout for these, for they provide the material for his own ideal. He also expects that, with the makers of these ideals, there is the possibility of a true community, a church outside the church and within the world. So, he seeks not only their ideals, but also their fellowship. Thus, the theologian has more reason to respect the material at hand. Yet, he still regards it as matter, as something to be regarded in general and vaguely as the opposite of his ideal.

ART

Art comes first among the examples to be considered here, and this is so not merely because Tillich finds it a most striking example of the interplay of form and substance but because these very concepts seem to belong preeminently to the domain of art or, more specifically, to Expressionist art. Tillich tells us that the definitions of these basic concepts "bear the impress" of the character of this art. If we recall that, for Tillich, all concepts, even a priori ones, enter our thinking through some concrete experience, then it should be clear how important this remark is. It amounts, at the very least, to an acknowledgment of influence. Fifteen years later, in his autobiographical work, *On the Boundary,* Tillich gives a fuller account of his intellectual debt to painting and especially to German Expressionism:

The discovery of painting was a crucial experience for me. It happened during the World War, as a reaction to the horror, ugliness and destructiveness of war. My delight even in poor reproductions obtainable at the military bookstores developed into a systematic study of the history of art. And out of this study came the experience of art; I recall most vividly my first encounter—almost a revelation with a Botticelli painting in Berlin during my last furlough of the war. Out of the philosophical and theological reflection that followed these experiences, I developed some fundamental categories of philosophy of religion and culture, viz., form and substance. It was the expressionist style emerging in Germany during the first decade of this century and winning public recognition following the war and the bitter struggle with an uncomprehending lower middle-class taste that opened my eyes to how the substance of a work of art could destroy form and to the creative ecstasy implied in this process. The concept of the 'breakthrough', which dominates my theory of revelation, is an example of the use of this insight.[58]

If we may take Tillich at his word here, then it would seem that the concepts of form and substance were derived by him through "philosophical and theological reflection" on his "experience of art," which was in part shaped by feelings of aesthetic delight aroused in him by looking at "poor reproductions" of paintings during the war, when he served as a chaplain on the western front, and by the even more profound feelings, revelatory in nature, evoked in him by a Botticelli painting in Berlin and by subsequent art historical studies, all of this against a background of the horrors of war and in reaction to them. But, it was through his encounter with Expressionist painting after the war, against the background of a revolutionary struggle against bourgeois sensibility and values, that he became aware of theological-cultural meaning of these concepts. This admission of influence, then, may lead us to expect that what we shall find in this brief example is more than a chance to see how the theologian of culture works but how the theology of culture was first conceived.

First of all, it should be noted that the theologian's concern is not with particular works of art but with a "trend" and with its general characteristics. "Trend" is a historical category and,

therefore, we should be reminded that, for Tillich, cultural-histor-
ical trends or general movements are best comprehended by
charting them on the culture line. The theologian of culture, then,
perceives movement when he looks at the material at hand, general stylized movement. In the case of painting, he sees a wild
movement away from naturalistic or objective representation. If
we were to take up his position and look with him, which we are
no doubt invited to do, we see the general form of a picture or,
perhaps, the general perspective of artists who have initiated this
trend in their work, so that what we perceive is a way of seeing.
We see content that has lost its meaning and nature naked,
"stripped of her appearance." 'Content' here denotes the scenes
of everyday life, ordinary objects and scenes, tangible and factual
things easily identifiable in their depictions, and 'nature' denotes
the background of all of this, a manifold of light and color and
soft shapes, that extends the scene indefinitely, giving it continuity with whatever we may want to turn to next, everywhere
and in all directions. No doubt, readers of this text are expected to
recall a remark in the previous section about the relationship of
form, content, and substance: "The shattering of form by substance is identical to content's loss of substantiality, to its becoming something nonessential," and an earlier remark that the shattering of form by substance is still form, paradoxical form. When
anything loses its substantiality or essentiality, it ceases to be an
entity in its own right, autonomous, worthy of respect. In that
sense, it suffers a loss of meaning. These earlier remarks represented the point of view of the theologian towards culture as a
whole. Now, in this initial example, they receive confirmation,
and perhaps more, their provenance is disclosed.

        To make clear that this artistic vision has more than aesthetic
meaning, Tillich recalls Schelling. The denaturing of nature dis-
closes the "ground of nature," the abyss upon which nature and
everything is precariously founded. This ground is not something
seen but a feeling or mood evoked by expressionistic images.
"But at the ground of nature, says Schelling, dwells dread." This
reference, I think, is to Schelling's *Philosophical Investigations Concerning the Essence of Human Freedom.*[59] One of Schelling's aims in
this work is to explain the origin of evil. Like Kant, he finds it in

an evil inclination in human nature, although his interpretation
of this inclination is very much un-Kantian. This evil tendency is
the ground or dark principle, not the "ground of nature," which
is a recurring tendency in nature towards chaos and disorder, but
a "higher ground," which is even more abysmal, the opposite of
the rational principle that enlightens and guides mankind. Consciousness of this ground or abyss causes "dizziness" and a desire
to plunge into its depths. It is a primal anxiety, "the anxiety of
life" (*die Angst des Lebens*), which drives man away from the
center of his being in the divine life and into a world of individuality, creatureliness, loneliness, irrationality, and death. This
willful act, however, is not merely an act of disobedience; it is
motivated by a desire to exist and, hence, is a self-positing act.
The motivation to evil is "the original ground of existence" (*der
Urgrund zur Existenz*), it is the desire for independent autonomous
existence apart from god. Creation and fall coincide. The origination of the visible world and the origination of human guilt are
the same event, or put simply, existence, which is self-inflicted, is
sin.

The general effect of Expressionist painting is to awaken in
us this dread or horror together with all of its metaphysical burden. I shall call this experience of "a form-annihilating No"
Tillich's "experience of art," or at least one element of it. To
Tillich, this experience is not only an experience of nothingness
but of substance, which resides at the deepest level of the self,
striving after form, and although its expression may be regarded
by some as cultural barbarism or a violent cultural anarchy of
forms consuming forms in behalf of the demon of creativity—for
example, Simmel, who attributed to Expressionist art a purely
destructive motive, destroying form "for the sake of flowing
formless life"[60]—Tillich responds that the No, which he admits is
the most prominent feature of this art, is merely preliminary to
the Yes. Both No and Yes originate in a ground of consciousness
deeper than any currently imagined. Speaking in behalf of the
artists, he goes on to say that their ultimate aim is affirmation. If
there is anxiety and guilt, there is also a will to redemption, the
conquest of existence, of willful individuality, and the endless
repetition of meaningless forms by a universal abstraction, the

abstraction of love, a mystical longing for the unity of all things. Expressionism, then, is essentially religious art, the sentiments and motives most characteristic of religion are expressed by it: primal anxiety, guilt, sin, redemption, love. And, this is confirmed by the artists' own interpretation of their work and by the statements of their "enthusiastic supporters." Their frequent reference to religious themes, even to the bible itself, is surely no accident. Here is content well-grounded in substance.

It has been observed by Michael Palmer, that Tillich's characterization of Expressionist painting and of painting in general, not only in this text but throughout his many writings about art, is related only tangentially to the paintings themselves and tends to lead us away from them and not toward them. We are not invited to look closely at the works themselves, to look closely at their composition, technique, etc.[61] This criticism might be deflected by Tillich by recalling that detailed criticism of cultural realities is beyond the scope of the theology of culture and unlawful. But Palmer's criticism is more serious than this. Tillich's fault is not that he is more interested in his theory of art than in artworks themselves and that he refers to artworks only in general, as instances of the validity of his theory. There is no fault in this. Rather, Tillich's fault lies in the fact that his theory does not seem to fit Expressionist art or any of the art he occasionally cites. At the very least, it conflicts with some of the major interpretations of Expressionist art by the artists themselves, by Kandinsky, for example. Consider his programmatic essay "On the Question of Form," first published in 1912.[62] The difference is not that Kandinsky is concerned only with art and not with life; the concluding comments of this piece make abundantly clear that this is not the case, as it was not with other Expressionist painters who wrote about their art.[63] The difference is twofold. First, for the artist, the spiritual meaning that painting expresses, its "sound" or internal content, which is evoked by the visual form, is expressed by the autonomous work of the artist and by the necessity effected in his work that combines outer form and inner spiritual content. Second, the meaning that is expressed here, so far as it can be expressed verbally, differs in content and in mood from the mythical elaboration of the No and the Yes that Tillich draws from Schelling. Kandinsky's meaning affirms the autonomy of the world. "The world sounds. It is a cosmos of spiritually effective beings. Even dead matter is living spirit."[64]

But, it is still possible that these artists misinterpreted their own work and that the theologian of culture is in a position to understand the meaning of their creations better than they themselves. The only way to settle a difference like this is to examine the works themselves, not, to be sure, in isolation but in their appropriate contexts, within human life, and within their proper domain, the art world. But, as Michael Palmer has shown, when one does this, one finds Tillich's interpretations not only barely applicable but misleading or false,[65] and while this does not make competing interpretations, even the artist's own, true, this failure on Tillich's part to illuminate the works themselves is sufficient to cast serious doubt upon his theology of art.

If Tillich, as a theologian of culture, has misrepresented Expressionist art, the very art that was supposed to have awakened in him the sense of reality that came to inform his understanding of culture in general and that one might expect he would understand best of all, is there not reason to suspect that the theology of culture itself has been ill-conceived? And, if it should turn out that the theologian's interpretation of painting is an alien interpretation imposed from beyond the autonomous domain of art, is it not, in spite of its vagueness and indifference, a heteronomous interpretation?

SCIENCE

Science here means philosophy of science and, in particular, the philosophy of science of neo-Kantianism. From the standpoint of the theologian, neo-Kantianism appears as idealized science. It is the perfect realization of autonomous reason, finite to be sure but a self-sufficient totality, something worthy of the highest intellectual respect, a respect that here seems almost obsessive. What must be perplexing to the theologian is that this perfect self-contained totality is pure form, a transparent sphere floating in intellectual space. It is without substance—which is what I take Tillich to mean by the attribution "unreligious." To him, it must seem as though another heaven has come into view, perfect but alien, wonderful but unaccommodating, necessary but unapproachable.[66] The disorder of the material at hand that the theologian perceives is not here but belongs to the "current thinking" about this perfect realm, thinking whose desire is to "get beyond" it. "Current thinking" must denote the motions of thought and feeling of those dissatisfied with perfect science and longing for the metaphysical substance of an older science that neo-Kantians, like their illustrious predecessor, had expelled from the domain of pure reason. They long for the "experience of reality," a reality that is not the mere construction of thought. Not concepts but a primal intuition—the direct apprehension of reality—is their preferred means of cognition. The difficulty that current thinking faces is all the greater because, for a while after Kant, "during the period of idealism," there was an inundation of substance, and the friends of substance then created, in the place of science, a new form antithetical to science. This new form, however, was not altogether new, it was the form of Christian dogma.[67] Over against secular autonomous science, they established a heteronomous religious science. The war between science and religion, which was waged during the period of idealism, was not caused by a conflict within reason itself but by an assault upon it from without by a heteronomous force, whose weapon was a "new form," doubtless a paradoxical form, "which in the name of intuition opposed the autonomous forms of science." Therefore, the friends of form had no alternative but to wage total war against the "materialistic shadow of Idealism," a curious expression whose meaning escapes me entirely. Their cause was just. But, they fought only a defensive war. They were satisfied when they had made their own domain secure, which they did with such a thoroughness that they would never again be in danger of another breakthrough by substance into their domain. Yet, the longing persists and has found expression in a historical movement, a "trend towards intuition." What should have been learned from the older conflict, however, and must not now be forgotten is that this trend should not be taken as an occasion to renew the conflict against science. If this trend, this longing for reality unmediated by science, be called metaphysical, then metaphysics cannot be a science.[68]

What does Tillich mean by 'intuition'? Is it intuition in science, in particular, in the sciences of thought? In *The System of the Sciences*, Tillich defines intuition as an attitude, basic to logic and mathematics, "in which knowledge examines its own immanent forms," in which "the object of knowledge is present in the process of knowledge itself."[69] But, this conception of pure intuition is hardly alien to Kantian formalism. Moreover, according to Tillich's system of sciences, logic and mathematics are not sciences of culture, not in the same way as a science of the categories. So, Tillich must mean something else. He means metaphysical intuition, the unmediated awareness of reality. Is this reality the unconditioned absolute meaning that is a quality of consciousness, or is it unconditioned being pure and simple? Tillich does not say, but the context gives every indication that he means the latter. If this is so, if Tillich means to say that there is an absolute reality that transcends thought, not, to be sure, a being but being itself, and that we intuit this reality, are directly aware of it, then he has departed in a very basic way from the principles of cultural science and has entered the realm of speculative metaphysics.[70] Of course, Tillich might respond, if we could question him, that he is representing not his own metaphysical beliefs but those belonging to the makers of this trend toward intuition, whose incursions into form he interprets as a sign of hope for the theonomous renewal of science but whose tactics he regards with some displeasure. We must not forget that we are dealing here with cultural science, with theories about meaning and not about reality outside the mind. And, for want of a better explanation, I am willing to accept this one and let the matter drop. After all, Tillich goes on to define metaphysics as a maker of paradoxical meanings, as experience, no doubt, mediated and not pure intuition of the unconditioned.

How does intuition gain access to modern consciousness, which has been shaped by a self-determining autonomous reason? Tillich's answer is that substance leads the way by bursting forms and preparing the way for a new metaphysical intuition. Which forms and where? Wherever, in the previous conflict, the shadow of idealism had been defeated and autonomy established. Thus, this incursion seems to involve all of the forms of science. But, if these autonomous forms are secure and perfect in their domain (the domain of rational self-consciousness) and if this domain is not itself subject to any internal conflict of reason with itself, if it is self-sufficient and diligent in observing its limits and never needs to open itself to a reality that is beyond it, then must not this path-breaking and form-breaking work of substance be subversion, infiltration, intellectual terrorism? If the friends of substance are wiser than their predecessors and will avoid open conflict knowing that they are no match for autonomy on the field of science, we might expect them to adopt a strategy of a protracted guerrilla war. This new struggle, which is not a conflict, takes the form of a revival of metaphysics that now is no longer said to be a science. The work of this new metaphysics, we may suppose, is not conceptual work but mythmaking, the fashioning of paradoxical forms, powerfully expressive, that subvert the claim of science to represent the whole of reality and are properly instruments of substance. What is metaphysics but "the paradoxical attempt to put into forms that which surpasses every form, the experience of the unconditioned." But, Tillich adds, today there is no great metaphysics. So, it is only natural that one would look back to Hegel. But, although Hegel evolved a profound synthesis of the No and the Yes of substance, his strong optimism made him unsusceptible to the experience of dread. So the unromantic, rationalistic Hegel must be supplemented by Schelling in his later period and by Schopenhauer.

This is a fanciful account, and while I admit to having made it seem even more fanciful in my presentation of it, I don't believe that I have been unfaithful to its content. As an account of the history of philosophy in Germany from Kant through the heyday of neo-Kantianism, however, it is not only fanciful but ludicrous. German idealism appears as the ravings of romantics intoxicated by the straight substance that Kant extracted from reason when he made it pure. But the perfection and the pure formalism of Kantianism is a naive myth. Tillich must have known well enough that the motivation of idealistic philosophers was for the most part directed by insights that came from Kant himself as well as from perplexities and inconsistencies in Kant's work, so that in large part they were carrying on what they took to be Kant's work. And, as Tillich also must have known, neo-Kantianism was not the unified science that it hoped to be but, in reality, was a set of conflicting viewpoints, with conflicting tendencies toward logicism and physicalism, on the one hand, and toward histor-icism, on the other, and never itself entirely free from the danger of skepticism. Just as, in the case of art, Tillich's construction pro-vides little insight into the actual art world, so here his cultural-theological analysis of science and philosophy provides little insight and also misleads. So far, the work of the theologian of culture seems purely self-serving.

ETHICS

With this last set of examples, our survey is complete in two senses. Not only will it bring the survey to a close, but it com-pletes it systematically. All of the mental faculties will have been represented: the aesthetic, the theoretical, and now the practical. Tillich offers three examples here, the first concerns individual or personal ethics, the second and third, social and political ethics. By individual ethics, Tillich means the ethics of personal realiza-tion. According to current parlance, his ethics is teleological rather than deontological. This is consistent with his theory of cultural-scientific standpoints and with his Fichteanism. The founding of a normative-cultural science is a self-positing act. In this way, and only in this way, the individual becomes a person. To be a person is the goal of every self-conscious individual, and one achieves this goal by an original act of self-creation upon the stage of history. Since Nietzsche figured so importantly in the account of this process discussed in the first chapter, it is not surprising that he should play a prominent role here as well.

Nietzsche's emphatic exclusion of religion from his stand-point is what attracts the theologian of culture, not because he views it as a threat but as an opportunity. The denial of religion will prove to be only apparent. His "doctrine of the formation of the personality" advocates an ethics of grace in opposition to an ethics of virtue. But, grace is one of several manifestations of substance, it is a paradoxical form, and an ethics of grace is one whose first appearance is marked by a "violent shattering of ethical forms." And, is this not precisely the effect of Nietzsche's teaching, his message? If Nietzsche preaches a message of grace, then he must do so from the standpoint of substance, which is to say he must be a theologian, albeit, a paradoxical one. If the pharisees and Rome be taken as advocates of conventional virtue, then Nietzsche may be said to belong to a line of religious teachers that includes Jesus and Luther.

The No and the Yes, the characteristic concepts of a theological standpoint, are foremost in his doctrine. Tillich illustrates this by quotations and references to Nietzsche's *Thus Spake Zarathustra*. First, he quotes from Zarathustra's preaching about the "hour of the great contempt," which is the greatest possible human experience, when the heretofore considered greatest human values, happiness, reason, justice, and pity along with virtue, are perceived with disgust. Virtue, the sum of qualities of the well-formed or cultivated person, counts as nothing because it does not make us rage.[71] This uncompromising judgment, which calls upon us to reject absolutely every value hitherto respected, is "the virtue that causes one to rage," which is "beyond virtue and sin" and is, in reality, the virtue of grace, or so we are supposed to infer. Likewise, Nietzsche's message is said to repeat "the theological judgment of nothingness" against the individual.[72] This is followed, "at once," by the Yes, by Zarathustra's preaching of the Overman, the one who is to come, and by his hymning, his love song to eternity and to the "nuptial ring of rings, the eternal recurrence."[73] Indeed, in the latter case, this is quite literally true. Zarathustra likens himself to a thundercloud moving "between past and future" heavy "with lightning bolts that say Yes and laugh Yes, soothsaying lightning bolts" and thus goes on to bless himself with a lordly blessing, "blessed is he who is thus pregnant."[74] The experience presented in Zarathustra's affirmation is of a reality that transcends the personal and, therefore, the virtues, which are conventionally taken to be the formed content of a cultivated personal life. Therefore, it is only paradoxically affirmative of personality and, therefore, Nietzsche must be perceived by received moral thinking as an antimoralist, pure and simple. But, this is just how they regarded Luther. Whoever thinks thus merely reveals that his own thinking about personal values has not transcended ordinary conceptions of virtue and reward. This last remark contains another allusion to Nietzsche's *Zarathustra*. Zarathustra hears the gentle voice of beauty, his "shield," speak the truth about those who are "expert on good and evil," that is, "the virtuous": she says, "They still want to be paid." This persistent desire is sufficient to condemn them, for what is supposed to distinguish virtue from other human motivations is that it is its own reward, and in the virtuous life this achievement should replace all other goals. Yet, those who live a virtuous life continue to seek some other reward: some demand retribution, punishment, and revenge against the wicked; others seek the pleasure of self-punishment; still others only desire easy living, that is, the relaxed conscience of those whose vices have grown weak, and so forth.[75]

Does Tillich mean then that only hypocrites condemn Nietzsche, along with Luther and Jesus, as an antimoralist? Or, is something more intended here? The next paragraph makes clear that something more is meant. To condemn Nietzsche is unavoidable for anyone who has taken the standpoint of form. There is somewhat of inevitability and tragedy in this condemnation. From this standpoint, the No and the Yes of Zarathustra's preaching is "absolutely paradoxical." But, from the standpoint of substance, it is the triumph of metaphysics—as characterized earlier as the paradoxical nonscience that strives to put the unconditioned in forms—over autonomous ethics. The effect of this triumph is "to deprive ethical contents of their relevance" or, as it is said somewhat differently in the next sentence, to make them relative, perhaps societally and historically, to shatter their forms—the form of unconditionality and universality that is the form of the moral law in general?—and to use these broken forms as vehicles of a higher metaphysical way of becoming a person. This new form of a person is of one who is "beyond good and evil," who is absolutely—that is, from the standpoint of substance—"better" (why not "best"?) even though, or perhaps just because, from the standpoint of autonomous ethics, he appears "worse" than the good and the dutiful (why not "worst of all" or "wicked"?). From the theologian's point of view, this new person exemplifies the paradoxical form of grace. But, one must ask, is this person the recipient of grace or the bestower of it?

What is content and form here? Does content mean the moral rules and maxims and the virtues that guide and train the soul? And what is form? Does it consist of universal moral principles, such as the categorical imperative, as well as such concepts as will and freedom, that from the standpoint of autonomy are formal and empty of any specific content and that, because in them alone resides the causality of moral acts, must be kept apart from sentiment or passion or other causal principles that do not originate in reason, such as grace? And, how is form shattered? In the first place, as noted earlier, it becomes disassociated from its conventional content, which is shown to be relative and often irrelevant to meet current moral demands. Second, it becomes empty because its purely formal qualities have been shown not to fit its content. Third, it is redefined from the standpoint of substance. Freedom is no longer autonomy, a faculty of rules, but is overwhelming creative power that seems to come from beyond manifest in new realizations, and that justifies when it is exercised at the greatest risk to the personal agent. And, the unconditionality of the moral law is no longer a logical principle but a deeply felt sentiment, a quality of consciousness.[76] But why should autonomous ethics agree to this radical transformation of its program, since it has its own normative program? And, if it is not compelled by some deeper dialectical necessity to agree—and Tillich has not shown this, although he undoubtedly assumes it— then the theologian has not overcome a divided consciousness in ethics. Autonomous ethics remains within its horizon, with its own forms and norms. The latter, of course, the theologian has blocked out of his vision.

But what about Nietzsche, can Zarathustra's message be interpreted fairly as an ethics of grace? If Nietzsche's attack upon conventional ethics represents a "trend," "current thinking" about a future that is coming, then here at least, outside the church, the theologian has discovered a form of the ethical life, which is expressive and which, therefore, fits the demands of substance. If paradoxical form is a criterion of an ethics of grace, then to this extent Nietzsche's higher ethics can be called an ethics of grace. But, perhaps, even grace must be taken in a paradoxical sense if Nietzsche's ethics is to quality completely: if grace be interpreted not as something received but something self-bestowed, if it be said to come not from the absolutely beyond but from the unlimited power of expression of the soul of the Overman who blesses himself, then Nietzsche's ethics might be called an ethics of grace. But this, I suspect, would be too paradoxical even for the theologian of culture. If so, then the radical trend that the theologian perceives and that seems to mirror his own moral point of view is really moving in a direction opposite from the one he would choose. Therefore, the theologian is faced with three and not just two conflicting ethical standpoints—autonomous ethics and two diverging "ethics of grace"—and, because they have entered into his consciousness, this moral view is all the more divided.

The theological analysis of social ethics has two parts: first, a consideration of social ethics generally; and second, a theological analysis of the state. Surveying current trends in social thought and social action from the standpoint of substance, the theologian perceives "everywhere a resurgence of love mysticism," a movement away from rationalized social existence back toward a community whose binding principle is love. Substance in the realm of social ethics is manifest as love. Noteworthy about this trend is that it is not limited to a particular community, it is not just Christians loving one another in a more exuberant way. It is happening "everywhere." Everywhere, there is evidence that this new moral spirituality has broken through "Kantian formal ethics of reason and humanity."[77] As agents of this new spiritual breakthrough, Tillich no doubt had in mind various and sundry anarchists and radical socialists. Tolstoy, in particular, advocated a Christian anarchism based upon Jesus' teaching in the Sermon on the Mount. Tillich's mention, in this context, of the poems of Rilke and Werfel, however, is puzzling, for while romantically exuberant no social doctrine founded upon love is to be found in them. His mention of "idealistic socialists and communists" whose speeches carried the new message of love,[78] sets this movement apart from Marxism and most notably from social-democratic theory and practice, which owed much of its inspiration to Kant.[79] Here also, the theologian seems to recognize only the formal validity of Kantian moral doctrine while ignoring, deliberately or not, its normative validity.

Yet Tillich's attitude toward Kantian ethics seems strangely ambivalent. On the one hand, he solemnly affirms the absolute inviolability of Kant's moral concepts: of the autonomy of the moral will, of the purity of ethical motivation, and of the categorical imperative. These concepts make up the foundation of "autonomous ethics," a foundation that can be shaken neither by divine prerogative nor by the power of love that is able to overcome the law. Is he saying too much here? Has he not just said that Kantian forms have been shattered, and does not substance have the power to convulse everything and rebuild it? And, what is the meaning of the metaphor that follows? If Kantian form is a vessel too small to contain the content, which is love, the new theonomous morality, then its inviolability only contributes to its isolation and irrelevance. Is this overflowing love still dependent upon Kantian form, or is it altogether independent? Independence might seem here to be the right answer.[80] And, just how does love surpass autonomous morality? Does love make demands upon us that exceed what is required of us by a morality founded upon pure practical reason, so that from the standpoint of substance, of theonomous ethics, Kant's rational morality must seem immoral just because it is indifferent to whatever, beyond the law, love requires? If the Sermon on the Mount counts as an example of the morality of love (and we have seen that at least Tolstoy's interpretation of it counts here), then this interpretation is correct, although the law that love surpasses in Jesus' teaching is not the law of rational morality but of convention that has made compromises with human weakness. Thus, love requires that we not only love our neighbors but also our enemies, that we do not seek retribution, that we give to our petitioners more than they ask, that we cultivate in our discourse the simplicity of truthfulness, that we train ourselves to keep our attitudes and desires consistent with right behavior. In short, it requires a more rigorous moral discipline. It should be clear that this is not what Tillich means. It should also be clear that this more rigorous morality is not inconsistent with Kantian ethics. Perhaps Tillich means by love that highest of spiritual gifts, of which St. Paul speaks in *I Corinthians*, Chapter 13, and without which all our good deeds would count as nothing. But a plain reading of that text shows that 'love', which is a gift of the holy spirit, denotes a moral character made up of several virtues: patience, kindness, lack of envy, modesty, gentleness, even-temperedness, forgivingness, truthfulness, moral endurance. But this is not what Tillich means by love, and, if he does, surely a Kantian ethics is not without a doctrine of virtue and not without these virtues.[81] However, the ethics of grace has already shattered the form of virtue, so love cannot be a virtue. Perhaps, the morality of love surpasses rational morality in the same way that the organic surpasses the merely atomistic and mechanical. Thus, in the final sentences of this discussion about social ethics, love makes its appearance as the No and Yes of substance. The world as a mere collection of particulars is denied, it is experienced as an empty shell. Individualism is denied, and utilitarian rationalism gives way to "the experience of pure being," which is love, which is a cosmos, a universe that affirms the reality of all things. But these sentences do not seem to represent anything recognizable in Kantian ethics. And, one wonders why love, as a caring for things, which is what is meant here, needs to be grounded in the experience of pure being?

Tillich's theological analysis of the civil state is more than one example among others. As he comments at the end of this section, the series of examples taken together outline a cultural-theological system. They project what is intended by such a science. Not only do the examples represent all of the functions of the mind, but in this last example, the whole of culture is taken up and passed in review in a comprehensive normative-theological vision. And this is fitting, because of all human organizations, the state is the most comprehensive. Thus, this review ends with a grand spectacle.

The analytic task of the theologian of culture is to point to the situation of substance in different forms of the civil state. If we represent the state as a garden, the substance is a plant growing within it that, as it were, either takes over and even "overgrows" the boundaries of the state or is crowded out by other plants growing there. These other plants that compete with substance for space in the garden may be taken to represent radically autonomous, that is, secular, cultural forms. The crowding out of substance must be interpreted as the exclusion or restriction by secular authority not only of historical religion but also of the possibility of spiritual realization generally. Exclusion of the latter is a consequence of a strategy to defeat the former. The autonomous state is a new regime founded by modern political rationalism to succeed an older theocracy against which it struggled and won. This new regime restricts religion in principle by its abstract formalism. In this instance also, the theologian descries a floating abstract form: "the abstract state hovering above society." It may be said to govern from a distance with detachment. Doubtless, Tillich has in mind the modern bureaucratic state. Once again, he refers approvingly to Nietzsche's *Zarathustra,* specifically to the section entitled "The New Idol." There, Nietzsche depicts the modern state as a great serpent, or as a cold blooded sea monster, Leviathan, who like the original serpent is a liar. It is the annihilator of peoples, and yet it claims for itself identity with the people. But, this is a lie. Only creators create people and rule them in faithfulness and love. Annihilators entrap masses in the state and rule them by means of assorted artificial pleasures and, finally, by the sword.[82] Hegel's attempt to overcome this harsh abstraction by clothing the state with the cultural functions does no good. Indeed, it does much harm, for this superficial clothing has the effect of capturing spiritual substance and making it an instrument to serve the interest of the modern state, which is power.

Over against this spiritual-life threatening power state, which is disguised as a benevolent provider and protector of human well-being or as an idealized culture state, there arises idealistic 'Anarchism'—the quotation marks are Tillich's, put there to suggest that anarchy is a paradoxical form of the state, and hence, in this time, just after the first World War, in a time of revolutionary ferment, the agent of substance that "bursts open the autonomous form of the state" and promises not a return to theocracy but the coming of a new theonomy. Anarchy, then, represents a negative political form, it is the No of substance. But, although he does not say so explicitly, it seems clear that Tillich intends it also as the Yes—for does not the Yes follow always immediately upon the No? Anarchy is the paradoxical form of a new human community, heir to the title 'church', a nonhierarchical federation of communities, each with its particular cultural function—for rationalism survives here at least so far as to maintain a division of labor. The paradox that Tillich finds here, then, is not in lack of organization but in lack of a head in which power resides, a rulerless state. The difference between a theocracy and a theonomous state is that, whereas in the former, god rules through a chosen vicegerent and power is wielded from above, in the latter, everyone participates in the spiritual power that unites the whole and there is no ruler. But, of course, this is what the term 'anarchy' means. And there is nothing inherently paradoxical about this, although many including Tillich may take it to be impractical. The paradox lies not in the form of anarchy but in the attitude of those who continue to hold to it as an ideal when they believe with good reason that it is unworkable.

In any case, questions of practicality are of no concern to the theologian of culture. His task is merely to point to the ideal and to signs that the power able to bring this about, the power of substance, which is his standpoint, is already manifest in the world. Others will bring this about, and the spiritual power of substance will work out its own course through them. The ideal itself is meant to prefigure a form of society that is theonomous but in which the autonomy of the cultural functions and domains is maintained, and this, no doubt, is what makes anarchy commendable. Since there is no ruler, power resides in the cultural communities, each with its own work and each with the right to define the method and scope of its work, and since the communities all share a common humanity, the work of each community serves all. Philosophers teach from what they know, and because their rationality has been spiritualized, the forms of their teaching express spiritual substance; artists according to their art create and direct the ritual acts that bind the communities together; prophets or moral visionaries create new values out of their own wisdom. These three communities correspond to the three intellectual faculties: cognitive, aesthetic, and practical; the two remaining communities, whose function is leadership and economic planning and management, complete this picture of the ideal state. Their functions may be said to represent lower faculties of the soul that have been transformed by the inflow of substance. Tillich does not say what kind of leadership would be required in such a state or how the goals, toward which the "bishops" of this spiritualized secular state lead, are chosen, whether they are the goals envisioned by the "prophets" or, what seems unlikely, some others. He has more to say about the last function. He envisions a socialist state from which the capitalist spirit has been banished and whose goals of production are altogether humane. And, because in any socialist ideal there can be no poor, for the concepts of the poor and of charitable giving have been "annulled on the soil of socialism," the functionaries who make up this community will oversee the fair distribution of wealth that belongs to all. Just as there are no poor in this ideal state, doubtless there are no masses who live in a state of alienation, so that these communities include everyone and everyone has his proper function. Thus, the ideal state is like a living being, a world motivated by a self-love that has been sublimated by a spiritual presence that dwells within it and that is the inexhaustible source of the state's best self-images. Love binds these communities together and fills their autonomous activities with spiritual substance, so that there is no longer any need for a special religious community or a special religious culture. Plato could not have done better than this. This ideal is envisioned by the theologian of culture from the standpoint of substance. The theologian, however, has no place in this ideal world, unless he assumes the anonymity of a world soul. His work has been divided among teachers, prophets, and priests. His fate, if it can be called such, is, like that of the demiurge, to be forgotten. Since he is without envy, this is altogether fitting.

Although the survey of examples ends here, Tillich concludes the discussion by explaining why this outline of theology is limited to culture to the exclusion of nature. Should there be a natural theology to complement a theology of culture? Traditionally, a theological analysis of nature amounted to a search throughout nature for evidence of divine wisdom, power, and goodness. The argument from design or, as Kant called it, the physico-theological proof is its product. This direct approach to nature, Tillich argues, is not possible, because nature becomes an object for us only through culture. It is by means of the activity of mind, which functions theoretically, practically, or aesthetically, that nature is made present as something objective. But this objective representation of nature is not nature in itself, which absolutely transcends the activities of mind. Tillich appeals to the Kantian doctrine of the thing in itself, which is never an object of knowledge but the limit of human cognitive activity. Yet, in his use of it, this doctrine takes on a mystical aspect, which, of course, Kant never intended for it. Tillich speaks of nature's "in itself," which like substance is expressed negatively and yet, also like substance, "gains reality for us only through culture." I am tempted to suggest that Tillich here intends to equate nature with substance, and I believe that this is not just fanciful but necessary, for otherwise nature would remain altogether alien to Tillich's idealistic system, a skeptical limit rather than a No that immediately becomes a Yes. In any case, natural theology as formerly practiced is excluded from among the theological disciplines; it presupposes the "mythology of 'nature in itself'," that is, the false doctrine that nature corresponds to what we imagine it to be in our reflections. The place of natural theology is taken by a cultural-theological hermeneutic of the experience of nature and of technology. It is not clear where natural science belongs in this scheme of things or whether it belongs at all.

5

We have seen in the second and third sections of the text that church theology has been deprived not only of most of its content but also of its own cultural sphere. Recognition of this loss and of the impropriety of trying to make up for it within the church has driven the theologian out of the church into the wide world of culture. Until now, however, consideration of the question, "What is to become of specifically religious culture?" has been put off. There is no place for it in the ideal state that the theologian has envisioned. The old religious functions are now performed by autonomous functionaries: poets and philosophers, moral teachers, statesmen, and economic planners. The answer to the question, therefore, seems obvious: the old religious culture, set apart and protected, must wither away. But, it is not so obvious to Tillich that this should happen, and his purpose in this final section is to explain why we cannot avail ourselves of this solution.

Briefly, Tillich's answer to the question is that a specifically religious domain of culture should continue separate from secular domains, whose life and work express spiritual substance and forecast a coming universal religious culture. And, this domain will persist for the time being or, rather, for as long as time lasts—an interim situation, to be sure, but one beyond whose end no human eye, not even the visionary eye of the theologian of culture, can see.

Tillich states that his answer to the question is implied in the polar relation between the religious and the secular as presented in the figure of the culture line. He then proceeds to develop his answer from this initial observation in what seems to be an argument of remarkable complexity and compactness. I may be mistaken in treating this as an argument. Tillich may have meant to offer only a derivation, but his derivation has all the telltale marks of an argument: premises, a conclusion, and logical form. So, I shall treat it as an argument. But it is complex; it divides into three stages, and I shall treat one stage at a time, following Tillich's order.

The first stage begins with the observation that although the religious and secular moments of the culture line are never separate in reality, they are separate, nevertheless, in abstracto, that is, conceptually distinct. The expression 'religious and secular moments of the culture line' needs clarification. Is it supposed to apply here to types of cultural reality and their tokens, a liturgy for the mass, a secular dance composition, monumental art, and such? Or, is it meant to refer to the basic principles of substance and form, which are present in varying degrees in every cultural creation? Tillich cannot have meant the former, for the whole point of the culture line is to identify types of cultural reality according to their distinct and discernible religious or secular or classical character, and these distinct discernible characters are supposed to be concrete and not abstract. What is more, the former interpretation of the expression contradicts the conclusion he is after, namely, that there are in reality—concretely and not abstractly discernible—separate and opposing spheres of religious and secular culture.

The second premise is an observation about the operations of the mind: our minds are governed by a psychological necessity in such a way that, in general, we experience things that in reality are joined only if we keep them conceptually apart. By 'things that in reality are joined', Tillich must also mean principles, in particular, substance and form. This interpretation, however, seems to contradict Tillich's earlier claim, in Section 3, where he introduced the figure of the culture line, that not only do we never experience pure substance and pure form but also we cannot conceive of them as being separate. "A form that forms nothing [i.e., that does not convey something substantial through its content] is just as inconceivable as a substance that is not situated in a form." Now, Tillich claims that we are compelled by some psychological necessity to separate principles conceptually in order to experience them, no doubt, concretely. But this contradiction may be only apparent, for in order to conceive of them as belonging always together, we must be able to keep them conceptually separate. These premises appear to be applications of Kant's theory of experience to the present issue: in every experience, we always subsume what is given in experience under a priori concepts or categories. These concepts not only unify the manifold for our understanding, they also separate and make identifiable certain aspects of this manifold. Without clear conceptual distinctions, then, our experience would be blind. But where does this put us in our progress toward Tillich's answer? The second stage of the argument does not answer this question but introduces something else for our consideration.

The second stage is a historicist argument. The concept of religion and related concepts would be inconceivable unless we were able to derive them from historical precedent. These concepts include, in addition to the concept of religion itself, religious values, such as holiness, sin, and grace; concepts of "the elements of religion," for example, myth, cultus, church. Likewise, the theology of culture would be inconceivable, as well as its task, which is to find religious expression in secular culture and to construct an ideal of a universal culture both thoroughly religious and thoroughly autonomous. If the concepts of religion are conceivable only on the basis of historical precedents, then at the very least there must have existed in the past and continuing into the present in some form a special sphere of culture that is characteristically religious. I assume that precedent entails a noticeable or noteworthy temporal duration. This conclusion does not imply that nothing is purely a priori in our concept of religion but it seems to imply that there is no religious a priori as such and that substance, which in Tillich's vocabulary is supposed to name the religious a priori, takes on a discernibly religious aspect only through the medium of some positive religious content. If this interpretation of Tillich's argument is correct—it is, of course, one that Tillich would not have wanted to accept—then the possibility exists of a universal culture that is thoroughly expressive but not religious, not even in the perverse sense of the demonic. But, I shall postpone further discussion of this to the last chapter. So, then, we would have no concept of religion unless there were, at the very least, a religious past of noticeable duration continuing into the present, or at least recoverable by us now, a special sphere of religious culture. However, this argument is insufficient to establish the critical content of Tillich's answer, that a special religious sphere of culture ought to be maintained. Recognizing this, he moves to the next stage of argument. Before following him, however, I take the opportunity to make an additional anticipatory remark. It is this: although religious concepts depend upon historical precedents for their meaning, it is possible to use them in new cultural situations with great expressive power and to experience through them values that are in no way religious. We now come to the third and final stage. For the sake of clarity, I shall restate the four premises given in the first two stages:

1. Although substance and form in reality never are separate, they are conceptually distinct.
2. Generally, and by virtue of a psychological necessity, we experience substance and form, which in reality never are apart, only if we keep them conceptually apart.
3. The concept of religion and other related concepts would be inconceivable unless we were able to derive them from historical precedent.
4. If the concepts of religion are conceivable only on the basis of historical precedents, then there must have existed in the past and continuing into the present a special sphere of culture that is characteristically religious.

The third and fourth premises together yield a fifth:

5. There existed in the past and continues into the present a special sphere of culture that is characteristically religious.

The third stage of the argument begins with the observation that precedent is not enough to bring about the conclusion that Tillich wants for his answer. What more is needed? Whatever it takes to show that this special sphere of culture that is characteristically religious and that has continued into the present with

somewhat diminished authority and through which the theologian of culture has derived his concepts of religion must not be
allowed to wither away. Why not? Has not the theologian of
culture rescued the religious principle from its special sphere of
realization and shown it to be everywhere operative, indeed,
wherever there is expression? Yes, but somehow even this
achievement is in danger unless that special religious sphere, the
church and its culture, also continues. But, I am getting ahead of
things. Having observed that precedent is not enough, Tillich
states another premise:

6. "We can experience the sacred as somehow distinct from
the secular only if we lift it out and set it in a special
sphere of cognition, prayer, love, and organization."

This proposition, I believe, was intended by Tillich to combine
Propositions 2 and 3 and, thus, to join the two lines of argument
together and move single-mindedly towards the conclusion. But,
let us consider it independently for a moment, as an answer to a
question that might be raised by someone who was listening to
Tillich's address: How do we experience that "quality of consciousness," which you associate with the religious potency or
substance, as religious in contrast to other qualities of consciousness that are secular? Tillich's answer is that we "lift it out"
and "set it in a special sphere" consisting of acts and creations of
the various mental faculties, which are especially expressive of
spiritual power, like prayer, mystical knowledge, love, and ecclesiastical order. That special sphere is the sphere of religion, which
we know exists and from which we have derived our concepts of
religion. But, from what is it lifted out? From the cultural world,
which may have contents possessing religious qualities but which
is not itself, as a world, expressive of spiritual substance? From
the wide world of culture? And, if so, how do we recognize it to
lift it out? By means of the conceptual distinctions that we bring
into play when we experience it in the first place. But, those
distinctions, substance and form, are concepts, forms that are not
inherently religious. The concept "substance" takes on religious
significance only if we interpret it in the light of religious concepts, the Yes and the No and such, which have been derived

from historical precedents. It is from these that we must "lift out" the sacred. So, we lift it out of a special sphere of the sacred that, as always, is embedded in a wider cultural world that itself is not inherently sacred. That the wider world of culture should have this secular quality follows from the fact that culture itself is the product of autonomous human action. What we lift out is the quality of the sacred—as we might lift out beauty from certain special experiences of art or nature—and, having lifted it out, we give it a general character and then we apply it to the same place or to the same kind of place. This is merely the process of empirical concept derivation, although we must not overlook the normative quality of these concepts. Our concept of the sacred, then, is a derivation from those moments in our historical past that are exemplary of a certain ideal or world view, that depict a normative vision, which on the one hand, includes aspiration toward some transcendent reality beyond the world, and on the other, views the wider world of culture, of which it is a part, as indifferent or hostile to its aspiration. Premise 6, then, is a revised statement of Premise 2, adding to the a priori concepts of form and substance, those religious-normative concepts that have been derived from historical-religious life. This all fits in very nicely with Tillich's theory of ideas outlined in the first chapter of this interpretation. So, let us return to the argument.

Armed with historical a priori concepts of religion and endowed with the universal concepts of meaning, the theologian of culture should be in a position to pick out religious expressions, or analogies of religion, in secular culture or wherever else they may appear. What need is there for a special sphere of religion? Tillich's answer seems to be that without it these religious expressions in secular dress or analogies of religion would disappear, or that, even if they were to appear, we would be unable to attend to them, or both. Indeed, both, for the two are mutually determinative: the inability of us and others to attend to the religious moments of culture would deprive us all of the ability to create culture that is religiously expressive, and the failure of us and others to create such culture would further weaken the general ability to attend to it. Propositionally, this amounts to the following assertion:

7. Our ability to experience the religious would cease unless there were a special religious sphere of culture in the world.

This proposition is the obverse of Proposition 6 and is true if 6 is true, and I believe that it is true. But, this is not the end of the argument.

The cessation of our ability would not be simultaneous with the disappearance from the scene of a special sphere of religious culture. One would suppose that both the cessation of ability and the disappearance of religious culture would be gradual with the former process extending beyond the latter, inasmuch as the nostalgia of individuals or groups often continues long after the decline and demise of human institutions and ways of life. Nostalgia creates nothing but ghosts. Since the theologian of culture, at any rate, cannot afford to lose the ability to attend to a religious expression in culture—without it he cannot fulfill his special vocation—he must do all that is necessary to maintain the vitality of special religious spheres of culture. Although, of course, he does not do this directly, but only indirectly. As we shall see soon, he relies on the church theologian, or the church theologian in himself, to do this.

What causes this loss of sensibility to religious expression? Tillich's answer is that the cause lies on the form side of the culture line. "Exact science, formal aesthetics, formal ethics, pure politics and economics claim our whole attention." What is the nature of this claim? It is the claim of reason, and its tendency to reduce everything to form. And, reason will have its way unless it is resisted with the greatest effort. Hence, the opposition and contradiction between religion and reason. And, how long must this conflict last? Tillich's answer is "so long as we are compelled to live in the sphere of reflection and not of intuition."

Let us consider for a moment this distinction between reflection and intuition. It is a distinction between two modes of cognition, the one discursive and mediated, the other speculative and immediate.[83] Reflection denotes acts of judgment by which we subsume what is given in experience under concepts provided by the understanding. We experience our world and everything in it in this way. Because concepts divide and separate, we can never achieve an experience of things in their totality and their essential unity. We could achieve this by intuition, which penetrates to the "in itself" of things, to their primordial essence, and to the underlying identity of all differences, but a "psychological necessity" keeps us from doing this. This necessity is the consequence of our having to live "in the sphere of reflection." (This is the same psychological necessity referred to in Proposition 2.) How long must we live in this sphere? Until the ideal of culture, envisioned by the cultural theologian, is realized. And, when will this be? The answer that Tillich would give is Never, that is, not in any temporal future. To put it another way, the sphere of reflection is the sphere of the fallen soul. So long as we dwell in this sphere— and I believe that Tillich thinks that ultimately it is not in our power to escape from it, although we can imagine escape routes, which is why he praises Hegel's metaphysics but disapproves of his optimism—we can only experience the religious and the secular in two opposing spheres of culture, the one richly concrete, and the other driving us toward empty form. The religious sphere of culture stands for intuition, although except in moments of "breakthrough," we can never claim to have such knowledge and, even then, there is mediation, so, at best, we can only imagine what intuition must be like. The secular sphere stands for reflection and for conceptual self-sufficiency, and of this, we know a great deal. Let us return once again to Tillich's argument. The conclusion, stated in Proposition 7 is still not the conclusion Tillich wants. Although we know that religious experience would cease unless a separate sphere of religious culture were maintained, we have not yet come upon the reason why we should want them to persist. But, a reason can be drawn from what has just been said. If, as Tillich charges, reason does tend to reduce all of our experience to empty forms, to abstractions—and we are to assume that reason has this effect even on concepts whose origin is not the formal endowment of the mind but concrete lived experience—and if, deprived of content, we no longer have the means available to us to direct us to the reality that alone is the source of meaning, value, purpose, and whatever else fulfills our highest and noblest aspirations, then we must, for the sake of our ultimate well-being, resist the claim of reason at all costs. But, we can resist this claim only by maintaining a separate sphere of religious culture.

    8. If we lose the ability to experience the religious, we also lose the ability to experience all those values and goals without which human life must remain unfulfilled.

    9. We must not allow the latter to happen.

   10. Therefore, we must not lose the ability to experience the religious.

   11. Therefore, we must struggle to maintain a separate religious sphere of culture.

Is Proposition 8 true? It is true if all that Tillich says about reason and reflection is true. But, how do we know this? How do we know that reason does not have other resources to develop meanings that fulfill, even religious meanings? How do we know that religious talk about intuition and its transcendent objects is not just the product of reflection, by which the thinking individual takes its bearings in an unfathomed and often disheartening world by imagining ideals that reflect his own and others' aspirations? And, how do we know that what comes to expression in the religious sphere is a power that is determinative of all the spheres of culture, so far as they are not merely autonomous forms but meanings that fulfill life? How do we know that concepts like "breakthrough," revelation, "paradoxical form," and "No and Yes" are not just the inventions of a well-endowed fancy rather than evidences of a metaphysical beyond of meaning? These are questions that will concern us in the next and final chapter of this interpretation.

Before quitting this discussion of Tillich's argument, some final observations should be made. This conflict between reason and religion is one between autonomy and heteronomy, for, as we have seen, theonomy actualized is always heteronomous. The theologian of culture is not free of this conflict. Indeed, it enters into his consciousness, which is divided thereby. On the one hand, he is committed to uphold the autonomy of the wide world of culture; on the other hand, he is dependent upon the narrower world of religious culture for the material from which he constructs his normative ideal. But this narrow world of religious culture, the historical Christian church, also is alien to him. We

saw earlier, in Chapter 3, that he was driven from this world
because its heteronomous claims were intolerable. For him, the
conflict is tragic and, like all good tragic conflicts, it is inescapable.
But, Tillich closes the first paragraph of this section with the
observation that the conflict has become less severe because the
cultural developments of the last few centuries—since the Renaissance?—"have taught us to see through it." What we see
through to which is beyond tragedy is not stated. Nor does Tillich
spell out for us just what developments since the Renaissance
have provided us with this insight. But one can guess, at little risk
of error, that he means the developments in philosophy in Germany after Kant, in which an attempt was made to restore metaphysical intuition to its place as the origin and source of all our
knowledge. The unity of form and substance that exists in every
actual cultural realization but that is dissolved by rational reflection mirrors a deeper and more profound unity that lies beyond
being.

Having disposed of the question of what is to happen to
religion so far as it constitutes a special sphere of culture, Tillich
now turns to the main theme of this final section, the relation
between the two theologies. Here, too, our key is the polarity of
the culture line. The theologian of culture and the church theologian stand at opposite poles, and although they may seem
opposed, it turns out that on closer examination they complement each other, which is to say, they are correlates.

What follows is an interesting interplay between the two
theologies. We begin with the standpoint of the theology of
culture, which is supposed to be our standpoint also. This has
been our standpoint all along, and from it we have observed how
religious culture takes shape within the wide world of culture.
"How, through the influx of substance into form, culture receives
in and for itself a religious quality, and how . . . in order to preserve and enhance its religious quality, it produces from itself a
specific religious sphere of culture." The theologian of culture
knows that this special religious sphere of culture has no "logical
dignity," which is to say that it has no special relation to any of
the mental functions. Its principle underlies all the mental func-

tions and their faculties but, just for this reason, religion has no special claim upon them. The dignity of a specifically religious culture is only "teleological"; it serves a purpose, and when that purpose has been fulfilled, that is, when the ideal of the theology of culture has been realized, then it will become superfluous at the very least. But, while the theologian of culture knows this, and we too, the church theologian does not. (We, of course, know even more than the theologian of culture; we know that an influx of substance into form need not result in something religious.) We now take up our position with the church theologian and share his point of view. For him, the special religious sphere of culture to which he belongs does not originate from the wide world of culture. It is not something humanly fashioned. It has its own history, a sacred history, one, no doubt, that traces its beginning from the beginning of time and the narrative of this history continues down to the present. Within its domain it develops its own cultural forms, each of which has its own history and tradition, which, as the church theologian sees it, is independent of all worldly influence. And this, Tillich observes, is as it should be. But, from the point of view of the church theologian, whose task, we may infer, is to identify and interpret the norms of this special cultural realm and fashion them into an ideal, we cannot decide about the relation between the two theologies. We cannot decide because there is not only one possible church theological standpoint but three, and only after we have considered these will we be in a position to decide. We shall continue to stand with the church theologian observing how he would regard the wide world of culture. However, there is an additional noteworthy feature about the point of view that we are about to take. In Chapter 2, we noted how the theologian, in order to escape the intolerable ill of a divided consciousness, which has become acute because of the contradiction implied in the concept of theological ethics, departs from the church and seeks a cure in the theology of culture. As we stand with the church theologian looking out towards the world, we are to imagine him as a potential theologian of culture and ask ourselves whether, from his type of standpoint, he might see a way from his own to a cultural-theological standpoint. That way, if it presents itself, becomes not only a way out but, as we shall see, a way back. In short, it becomes the relation that Tillich is looking for.

Here, too, the culture line will guide us. What church theologians may not know, but what the theologian of culture knows and, perhaps, also the philosopher of culture, who should know something about the culture line as the a priori of cultural formation, and, of course, what we know, is that there are three and only three possible types of cultural formation and this means only three types of church and three types of theology and, therefore, only three types of attitude that the church theologian may take toward the wide world of culture, and toward the theology of culture, since that is where the cultural theologian dwells. It should be recalled that Tillich's construction provides for three types of cultural realization: a religious type, in which substance predominates; a secular type, in which form predominates; and a classical type, in which there is a harmony of form and substance. The three types of cultural realization to be presented here, however, are all on the substance side of the line. This presents no difficulty. A typology is a recursive schema and can be used repeatedly, although perhaps not ad nauseum, in its generated subdivisions, to produce more possible types. The three types in question, then, are all religious types. They all include theonomous ideals, but becaue theonomous ideals become heteronomous when realized, they are also three types of heteronomy.[84] Tillich does not rely solely upon this formal construction to develop possibilities, but consistent with his procedure of forming ideas, he also draws on historical precedent.

The first type is "typically catholic." Its ideal is of a universal church, a kingdom of god on earth that sets out to conquer the world, or, rather, it condemns the world and sets about to create its own counter world. All of its cultural realizations are absolute, incomparable exemplars of truth, beauty, and moral goodness. From here, there is no way out and no way in. The historical precedent that informs this type is, no doubt, the dominant form of Western Christendom from Constantine until the Reformation.

The second or old protestant type represents religious formations that flourished in Europe from the Reformation through the

Enlightenment. This type does not make absolute claims for all that is formed within it. Tillich's remark that "church, cultus and ethics are set free" means, no doubt, that autonomous cultural influences are acknowledged in their formation, and on account of this influence, their relativity with respect to changing fashions and styles in the way of the world also is acknowledged. Yet, absolute authority is claimed for dogma. Dogma is inviolable truth, absolute science. This claim is inconsistent, and its inconsistency can be shown in the following way. Dogma does not exist in its own right. It must always be related to its bearers or supporters, which in this case is the church and its functionaries. But the church has been acknowledged to be not an absolute institution but a historically relative one. It is not possible for absolute knowledge to be born out of a relative human group. Why not? Here Tillich's mention of the "theology of the Enlightenment" may be in order. It is not clear what reference is intended, but certainly Lessing should be counted here. According to Lessing, dogma was not absolute but instrumental in the shaping of the human race. The interpretation of dogma is an expression of the moral self-awareness of its bearers, and as this changes, so does dogma.[85] The overturning of this claim of absoluteness may give the theologian reason to seek an escape, but once out, there would be no return.

We come now to the third type, which has no precedent but whose discovery is the task of "present and future protestant theology." The task of present protestant theology is to create a standpoint that includes at its opposite pole the theology of culture. This and this alone will ensure it a creative future. This theological standpoint will adopt the theory of religion developed by the theologian of culture. It will distinguish between religious principle and actual religious culture and assign absoluteness only to the former. At the same time, the church theologian who fashions this standpoint, unlike the theologian of culture, will work actively and directly to create a sphere of religious culture. Also unlike the theologian of culture, the church theologian will maintain continuity with past theological and ecclesiastical traditions, selecting and reshaping what it receives from its traditions but always following a rule of continuity by reformation and of the continuity of the Reformation. He is not a revolutionary who seeks to found the new on the broken foundations of the old. Tillich claims that this is the only type of theological attitude that can relate positively with the theology of culture. It is certainly the only type left, if we accept his construction that only three types are possible, and the other two hold out only the possibility of a negative relation. But something more is needed in this standpoint in order to establish a positive relation. It is not enough that the church theologian acknowledge the relativity of his own stand-point and his own religious culture, nor is it enough that he allow himself to be influenced by a theory of religion developed else-where. He must also believe that religious realization is possible outside of the church, for otherwise he could not acknowledge the theologian of culture. But, if he believes this, why should he want to remain a church theologian and why should he be so solicitous of the continuity of his historical community and its traditions? And, if he understands the theologian well enough for there to be reciprocity between them, must he not then also understand and accept the validity of the cultural theologian's rule that direct creation of religious culture is heteronomous? His acknowledg-ment of the relativity of his norms does not make them less heteronomous, although it may temper their heteronomy or ren-der it harmless. Perhaps, the church theologian remains in the church because the cultural theologian needs him, but if for this reason, then he makes a very great sacrifice, for is he not con-demned, or self-condemned, to live with a divided consciousness, the very state that caused the cultural theologian to flee the church? And, would he not become all the more bitter if he were to look out from his situation into the wide world of culture and see the cultural theologian free and single-minded? But, before we explore this perplexity, I want to record some reflections about the three types of church theology.

I have assumed that the three types of church theology were derived by Tillich from his basic construction of the culture line. If this assumption is correct, how, then, do these three types ar-range themselves on the culture line? I assume that we must arrange them triadically, with two occupying each extreme and a third at the center.[86] Thus, we may locate the catholic type at the form side of the line, for although it opposes the wide world of autonomous culture with heteronomous power, nevertheless, it seeks to become omnicompetent and to include within its domain all types of cultural realization. In this respect, it mimics worldly empire. But, it cannot contain what it has consumed. The old protestant type stands at the substance pole. It lets the world have its due but it reserves for itself the domain of truth, and even though its dogma should become empty of substance as its content grows more and more irrelevant to modern scientific concerns, it may still restore its vitality from time to time through violent heteronomous outbursts. However, present and future protestantism, as it is represented here, does not take its place as a classical formation at the center of the culture line—we have already seen that Tillich had no taste for the classical—but as a transitional one preparing the way for the theology of culture and, in this role, it remains as a constant resource for the cultural theologian and a place to which he can return.

So, let us return to the two theologians. The theologian of culture is not confined within the church. His spirit is free and he roams the wide world of culture, open to its shaping influence and to every new form of life generated there. He is friend to artists and philosophers, poets and scientists, social and political visionaries. He moves in their circles and witnesses the flourishing cultural anarchy that presently rules the world and that provides him with the material for his own cultural ideal. Even the concrete forms that he receives from his own special religious tradition and that, Tillich says, he requires for his spiritual nourishment do not restrict him, for he can always enlarge their scope and alter them. I take this to mean that the theologian of culture is not bound by orthodoxy and is free to use whatever means are at hand to derive new meanings from old forms. He is unconcerned about the continuity of his native tradition. He has absolute hermeneutical liberty. He is not a maker or maintainer of traditions. This characterization, however, strikes me as inconsistent in a number of ways. First, the theologian of culture may be free in the sense that the whole world is open before him to take into his gaze, but his freedom is somewhat illusory, for the one thing that he cannot do in this world is to create, or at least, create directly. Thus, he wanders about the wide world as someone who is hardly there, for he cannot enter wholeheartedly into any of its activities. He is a nonparticipant or, at best, a "participant observer." Second, if the claim made at the outset of this section and defended by lengthy argument was made by the theologian of culture, then he cannot be indifferent to the continuity of any tradition, although that argument does not make him solicitous of any one tradition more than of others. Third, if he is nourished spiritually from his native tradition, then his indifference to its continuity must make him not so much carefree but recklessly careless. Perhaps, this account is not about how the cultural theologian actually lives or even how he sees himself but how he appears to the church theologian, who is responsible for present and future protestantism and who, like the older brother in Jesus' parable, resents his brother's freedom and his own bondage to duty. Or, perhaps, Tillich was just carried away by the romance of the theology of culture or perhaps by ambivalence. In any event, the cultural theologian comes to himself and acknowledges his dependence. Perhaps, the sudden recognition that he is "in danger of becoming a fashionable prophet of an essentially doubtful and ambiguous cultural development" gives him pause. It is not hard to imagine that this danger should especially threaten a creative visionary who does no work but who creates indirectly.

And so the theologian of culture returns home, to correlation with his other self. Once again, we must employ the culture line, for there is not only complementarity in this relationship but opposition or, at least, the appearance of it. I have written 'other self' because Tillich tells us that the correlation of the two theologians and their theologies is best achieved in a single person. Two natures in one person seems appropriate for someone who bears in his imagination a vision of the world to come. We must examine this relationship more closely. If it is "best" to have two theologies in one person, why is it not to be desired in all circumstances? Perhaps, it is best for theology as such, or for the higher theology to come, that these two be together, but it is not best for either as independent forms of theological existence, for the "type of each," so that from time to time it may be desirable to separate them if they are to flourish. This must mean that, at least on occasion, each one restricts the other, affects it heteronomously, that as types, there is a basic conflict between them. And, of course, this is so because, as correlates, they occupy different poles of the culture line. Which one stands for substance and which one stands for form? If the theologian of culture is in danger, on occasion, of becoming merely fashionable, then, perhaps he stands for form. What, after all, is fashion but the mere similitude of form? And, then, the theologian of culture also is the guardian of autonomy. But, aside from this formal condition of opposition, what other reasons might there be to cause the two to conflict? If one wants his freedom in the world and the other is duty bound to maintain a tradition that, notwithstanding modern criticism and interpretation, is still an ancient tradition, then it is the opposition of a divided consciousness. Tillich says that the opposition cannot be a real one because the theologian knows that he needs the tradition and the church theologian knows that the tradition that he must maintain is of only relative and not absolute validity. But, these respective recognitions do not strike me as able to mitigate the conflict and even less to cut it off at the root. Quite the contrary, they seem bound to heighten it. For if the culture theologian wants freedom but cannot have it, or can have it only if he returns to the bondage from which he fled, and if the church theologian seeks absolute security in a continuing tradition but cannot find it there, yet must serve this very tradition that can give him no satisfaction, and if each reminds the other of what he does not have, then one cannot be a theologian in this world without enduring the greatest intellectual unhappiness and suffering inner conflicts that no one would choose to endure. But, this is best for theology. And so, we return to the paradox that I introduced earlier. If a divided consciousness is universally repugnant and if it is best for theology that the theologian have a divided consciousness, then what is best for theology is universally repugnant.

But, perhaps, what is best for theology is best for everyone. We have not yet reached the conclusion of Tillich's address. The theologian of culture who is also in his own person the present and future protestant theologian sees, by virtue of his ideal, beyond the division of the two theologies, but not necessarily beyond the opposition of the poles of sacred and profane. The ideal is not so transcendent that it is beyond the sphere of reflection. Conceptual distinctions still are the order of the day, even conceptual distinctions that draw their content from historical precedent. I assume that, for Tillich, the distinction between sacred and profane is one of these. Visions are not intuitions but only the promise of them. But, it seems strange that the ideal of the theologian of culture should not look beyond this opposition also. Does not the demand for a unitary culture, one that in all of its domains expresses a unitary substance, a single religious spirit that comprehends all and that in its continuity embraces all of historical time, the whole history of culture, also require the dissolution of the antithesis of sacred and profane? As long as the ideal does not require this, does not the danger persist, if it is realized, of a renewed outbreak of the war between autonomy and heteronomy? And as long as this division holds sway, the possibility of conflict between the two theologies must exist as well, for the one will want to remain within the precincts of sacred culture, while the other makes its home in the secular world. How, then, will the opposition between the two theologies be annulled? Tillich tells us that the opposition between them, "is only the expression of a culture that is divided between substance and meaning." One would have expected to read "between substance and form," for substance is supposed to be "the absolute actuality of meaning," so far, to be sure, as it is conveyed to consciousness by a formed content. In any case, so long as the opposition between sacred and profane continues, there cannot exist a unitary culture, or at least one that is not threatened with dissolution by the virtuosity of form or by the shattering effect of a powerful explosion of substance. But these questions are beside the main question of the theologian's distress and why it is best.

One might have expected, when the two theologies entered into polar opposition that a third form of theology would appear, and indeed this seems to be the case, although I hesitate to claim that Tillich intended it. He speaks of a "new cultural unity" in which the opposition of the two theologies has been annulled, which implies that something new has come. Unlike the ideal described in the last section, this new unitary culture has a place

not only for a theologian but for a particular religious community, within the greater cultural community, an "ecclesiola in
ecclesia." Out of this community, which is continuous with his
native tradition, the new theologian works, and everything in the
wide world that he finds to be religiously expressive he replants
and cultivates "on the soil" of this community. And, what arises
from this work is a self-renewing sphere of religious culture,
which is not opposed to the world but becomes its very center
and heart. Its rhythm is the never failing life beat of the whole of
culture. There is no instability in this new theology or in this new
culture, for the effect of the theologian's work within the new
religious community is to place the resources of religious expression beyond the realm of chance, which would reign if the
fate of religion were left to the creative anarchy of secular culture.
(So much for confidence in the validity of one's own visions!)[87]
One may assume that, once this ideal has been envisioned, the
theologian of culture will have completed his work of indirect
creation and will become free to enter the world as the new
theologian who directly creates the core of a coming unified
culture. It is for the sake of this theology and what will be accomplished through it that the theologian of culture endures the pain
of a divided consciousness, and it is best that he suffer this, for
what he has accomplished, we may suppose, is best for the whole
wide world. One cannot help but wonder why this ideal of a
religious culture should be immune, if realized, from the heteronomous consequences of every religious culture with univer-
salistic pretensions? Does not the chance mention of chance in
this summing up of the role of the spiritualized church in the
theologian's ideal reveal the same anxiety that is often, if not
always, the cause of the quest for spiritual power and security? It
seems as though the theologian of culture has suffered a failure of
nerve.

Tillich concludes this section and his address, with some
remarks about the role of theological faculties, so far as this may
be redefined from the standpoint of the theology of culture. In the
course of doing this, he recapitulates much of the content of his
address. Here, he speaks mostly not of ideals that may come to
pass but of work now to be done, and he ends by sounding the

call for attack against the powers that oppose religious realization. The work of the theology of culture, and of theology generally, is carried out, in Germany at least, by the theological faculties of a university. These faculties are not trusted by their university colleagues, because, traditionally, they presuppose that the object of their science is a being, namely god, and because their inquiries into the nature and existence of this being are restricted by the authority of confessional bodies that are outside of the university. The presence within the university of theological faculties holding these presuppositions threatens the autonomy of science and is an obstacle to the realization of the systematic unity of knowledge, which is the ideal of the university. Thus, it is understandable that the secular faculties should reject the theological faculty as an organism rejects alien matter. But, all suspicion should cease once it has become clear that theological faculties do not subscribe to the authority of alien bodies and do not presuppose as their proper object a supernatural being. When it is known that theological faculties merely stand for one standpoint among others, for which they claim no absolute truth (for cultural standpoints are neither true nor false) and that the object of their study is just these standpoints, which together comprise the sphere of religion within culture, that is to say, when it is known that theology is just one cultural science among others, in this instance, the normative science of religion, then there should be no objection to having a theological faculty within the university. Such an argument might be made today in this country for religious studies in public universities. Yet, one wonders whether this benign and curious phenomenon of modern cultural science is not fashioned to become a Trojan horse. For this interpretation of theology as the normative science of religion is merely a stage on the way toward the theology of culture, which, when it enters the self-consciousness of the theological faculties and directs their thoughts, lifts the goal of their aspiration high above their former dignity as one faculty among others, like law or medicine, to the same level as philosophy, which presides over all cultural domains. Today, for good or for ill, such a dignity is rarely attributed to philosophy even by philosophers much less to theology. In any case, it is Tillich's expectation, or at least his hope, that theological faculties that practice the theology of culture will rise to a new eminence and respect and will "carry out one of the greatest and most creative tasks within culture," which is to unify culture by restoring religion to a place at the very heart of the cultural life. Those who have advocated the removal of theological faculties from the university are liberals, whose ideal of culture is antithetical to the view presented here, and socialists, who fail to see that their aims and the aims of the theology of culture are essentially the same. Both religion and socialism oppose the liberal individualistic interpretation of autonomy that fragments culture and destroys community. There is a natural alliance between religion and socialism, and once this is recognized, the theologian may become the ideologue of "the new cultural unity that is arising on socialist soil."[88] The address ends on a militant note. For two hundred years, theology has been in retreat, abandoning one indefensible position after another. Now is the time to attack and "under the standard of theonomy" to reclaim all of the cultural territory that was lost to the infidel secularizers. However, the purpose of this battle is not to defeat autonomy but to set it free.

6

In the beginning, when I started to think about how this interpretative essay should be arranged, I was disappointed that Tillich's address consisted of only five parts. It seemed fitting to me that a work whose principal theme was the creation of a world should consist of six parts. If that had been so, then this epilogue, indeed the whole of my essay, might have been written as a sabbatical celebration of a good and perfect work. However, Tillich wrote only five parts—a mere failure of form that could easily be made right. For what is one day more or less? But, his work suffers from more serious imperfections, structural flaws, that threaten the integrity of the whole. To put it briefly, Tillich's system is self-defeating. But, if this is not providential, it is at least fitting. We all live in the sixth day. It is our present in the scheme of things, an unending but not an eternal present. We still have our labor. The future, which is always ahead of us is the sabbath in which we hope to find rest for our souls and, for our always restless minds, fulfillment in perfect praise. The sixth day is the day of our creation, for we were made on this day, our kind, female and male, in the image and likeness of god, so that in our self-awareness the world might become an articulate and interpreted whole. But what becomes is always becoming. Creators—and we are all creators—must always contend with what went before them, and they must work with the awareness that theirs is not the final creation. Moreover, the work of construction, which takes from this past and would be nothing without its precedents, not always but most often must begin with deep criticism and, in some sense of the term, with deconstruction.

The claim that Tillich's theology of culture is self-defeating needs some elaboration. A theory or system is self-defeating when failure in its use is due not to external circumstances and not to the incompetence of its user but to the application of its own principles.[89] Failure in this case means failure to reach the goals the system was designed to serve. In what ways, then, is Tillich's theology of culture self-defeating? In many ways, I think, but I shall review only the most prominent ones that have come to light in previous chapters. In the most general way, the theology of culture is self-defeating because it is inconsistent, because it generates contradictory assertions. Any system that does this is self-defeating because it can make no assertion without admitting the truth of its contradictory. While there is no doubt that such systems may serve the ends of unscrupulous persons with ambitions of unlimited power and control over their fellows by providing them with occasions to make arbitrary, self-serving judgments that, in the midst of confusion, appear to be in the interests of all, it is obvious that inconsistency is not a quality that is permissible in a system put forward with a good will and, therefore, always supposed to be subject to rational appraisal. And this, I think, unquestionably applies to Tillich's system and to his intentions regarding it.[90] If, therefore, we find that it generates contradictions, then it becomes necessary to revise it.

But the theology of culture is self-defeating for another reason. It has incompatible goals. The goals of Tillich's theology of culture are represented in its ideal. The chief of these is the realization of a culture that is thoroughly religious. In Chapter 4, we saw that the theologian's ideal envisions a culture in which there is no church, no special sphere of religion, no theologian, and no theology as a special discipline. I shall call this the pure or anarchic ideal of the theology of culture, in contrast to the impure or imperial ideal presented in the final section of Tillich's address, which locates a special sphere of religion and theology at the very heart of the ideal, its "holy of holies." Certainly, the pure ideal provides the best opportunity for harmony with Tillich's other aim, which, even though it is secondary, is not to be compromised. This is to preserve and enhance the autonomy of the cultural functions. Tillich believes that the secondary aim depends upon the primary aim. Why does he believe this? His answer, generally, is that the autonomous faculties of the mind create only forms that are at best representative of their own formal self-sufficiency and virtuosity but that they lack the power to embody these forms in content in such a way that they might become expressive of ultimate meaning, such as the theologian envisions in his ideal. And yet, unless they express meaning in this way, they remain unfulfilled. Lacking this, human life, lived autonomously yet requiring meaning if it is to be fulfilled, is subject to violent incursions of spiritual power against which it has no defense. For its own protection, as well as for its fulfillment, autonomy must subject itself to the higher authority of theonomy, which will respect its rights and through its ideal provide autonomy with access to the spiritual substance that it requires but lacks, or to put it another way, autonomous form must be infused by theonomous substance and the whole of culture must become explicitly and unambiguously religious.

However, there is reason to suspect that this harmony of goals is not so well established. To justify his claim that autonomous form needs theonomous substance, Tillich repeatedly, but not consistently, denies the capability of the autonomous faculties of the mind to fashion adequate norms consistent with their functions. Thus, for example, he denies that moral thinking has the capacity to envision the ideal of a society in which the ethical life might find fulfillment. He denies this in Section 4, even though it was precisely the right of autonomous moral philosophy to choose its own normative correlate, which may or may not be religious, which convinced the theologian that theological ethics was impossible. But, it is obvious that autonomous thinking has the capacity to fashion for itself such norms. Kant's ideal of an ethical commonwealth is one, Rawls' "full theory" of the good is another.[91] Neither ideal is religious, although Kant presents his ideal within the context of a moral reinterpretation of religion. I introduce these here only as examples of the capacity of rational thinking to develop secular ideals that have expressive power and that evoke life-fulfilling sentiments. There is no evidence that the capacity exemplified by these ideals is in any way less than the capacity of the theologian of culture to envision ideals from the standpoint of substance by intuition or ecstatic insight. And, as secular ideals, they, like any other rational product, are altogether public and entirely subject to rational appraisal. If, then, there exist secular ideals that offer the prospect of a unified culture under some principle of good, then the question at issue is not between a theonomous cultural ideal or no ideal at all, which is the way Tillich has set things up by denying to autonomy an original capacity of ideal world making, but between an ideal that is explicitly religious and others that are not. I say explicitly religious in spite of Tillich's claim that theonomy does not stand for a particular religious point of view but for the religious principle itself, because, by his own admission, all universal cultural principles reflect a particular historical origin. But, if autonomous reason has this capability, then it has no need to subject itself to a higher authority. And, if there is no need, then to claim that there is one becomes, on Tillich's terms, an arbitrary and heteronomous act. Tillich's strategy to save autonomy seems like the attempt to save a perfectly capable swimmer at sea during shipwreck by first disabling him.

If in order to maintain his ideal of a religious culture, Tillich must deny to autonomy capabilities that it does indeed possess, and if, on the other hand, in order to preserve and enhance autonomy, he must deny to the religious principle the right of universal domain, then his goals are incompatible. He may favor one at the expense of the other, or he may compromise both. Whatever course he chooses to follow will end in self-defeat.

The incompatability of the goals of Tillich's theology of culture becomes even more apparent when one reflects upon the nature of the religious principle itself, which is at least potentially the basis of all meaning and which, whether according to the pure anarchic ideal or the impure imperial one, is supposed to find expression in every cultural realization. What is this principle? It is the No and the Yes, which we have already noted is a very abbreviated version of the scenario of sin and justification. It is on the basis of this principle that the autonomy of culture is to be rescued. This "disguised norm" derived from the experience of sin and justification by grace is made by Tillich into the absolute ground or actuality of meaning. How does it work? How does it give meaning? Let us think about the doctrine more concretely. According to it, no human action, no work that satisfies a mere law, or a life lived consistently in this way, can make a person right or acceptable in the sight of god. This is because existence, that is, the state of being of individuals whereby they are separate from their transcendent ground, is sin and good works, while themselves not sinful, increase sin because they promote independence and cause self-confidence or the false consciousness of autonomy in existence. And this is true of everything that exists, singly or collectively, of a world or an individual. Good works cause "boasting," the false belief of human self-sufficiency, which entails a denial of god, who is the transcendent ground of existence. The "sight of god" is the standpoint of theology, the standpoint of substance. "Good works" are the activities and productions of the life of the mind. They are the actualities of culture in its various domains. Form corresponds to the law that increases sin. The No is condemnation, the theologian's critical judgment that human cultural productions are empty of meaning. It is also, more vigorously depicted, the form-shattering appearance of creative power that first destroys the self-sufficiency of forms. The Yes is grace beyond the No, which alone gives meaning to life and its activities. Its presence is best observed in those shattered paradoxical forms that are still forms. Cultural life, that is, life lived autonomously, unavoidably increases sin, and it is only made right by grace. But if this is so, then every autonomous creation is right only by virtue of a principle that is other than the autonomous formative principle itself. But, if the principle of right does not reside in autonomy itself, then it resides elsewhere and it is an alien principle. Thus, consistent with the religious principle, autonomous works are judged right only when they are made subject to an alien principle, that is, only under a heteronomy. But heteronomy and autonomy are incompatible. Perhaps the theologian of culture should abandon the claims of this religious principle out of respect for autonomy. But, he cannot do this. Even the theologian of culture must maintain continuity with his concrete theological circle and with the theological precedents that inform it. If he were to turn away from this, his identity as a theologian would be in jeopardy.

This introduces a third and more precise sense in which the theology of culture can be said to be self-defeating. Theology is a vocation that one undertakes, or should undertake, for a high purpose. In this it is like the law, or teaching, or politics, or medicine, or any other profession that serves the common good. Theology, therefore, is not merely a theory about reality. It is a practical science. Its purpose is to make things better or to prevent them from becoming worse. Just as medicine is supposed to promote health and law, justice, so theology is supposed to promote spiritual well-being, to enhance life. Suppose it were concluded by a select panel inquiring into the adequacy of the medical profession, that the current practice of medicine actually defeats the goal of promoting health, makes it worse, and that central to this failure is the illusion, under which both physician and patient live, that perfect health is an attainable goal. And, suppose that new attitudes toward health must be developed consistent with this new realism, in which the physician must become in appearance what he has always been in fact, not a wonder worker or a purveyor of medical grace but a technician working against unconquerable uncertainties, an experienced counselor who helps the patient attain objectivity towards his own state of health, and the patient must become more than a mere sufferer of ills, a responsible agent whose participation in healing is indispensible. Then the current practice of medicine would be self-defeating, and it would remain so until new ways were introduced. Suppose knowledge of these findings were confined to a very few and that its present esoteric form—a form that was deemed necessary to maintain, at least for the interim, the authority of the profession—were such that even if it were made public, few would understand its implications and many, finding it discomforting, would resist what little they did understand. Comforting illusions are difficult to dispel, and one does not come easily to a conception of a world where chance determines so much that is important to us, where we can be certain only that we shall never be free from the threat of illness and that someday we shall die and that ideals are valid only if we do not expect them to make us any metaphysical promises. These recognitions require a state of maturity that the medical profession has not heretofore promoted. Then, as these findings and their implications gradually become known, physicians would be faced with very difficult choices. The findings might confirm suspicions that their professional self-image and their professed ideal are incompatible. Yet, in many instances, they continue to practice their profession with satisfactory results, and many of these successes they attribute to the public confidence in their special reserve of skill and knowledge. The revolutionary changes proposed would be sweeping; the public would be slow to understand them; many would become disoriented and, consequently, easy victims of the lure of less responsible wonder workers whose promises of health appeal more directly to basic anxieties. Even to attempt a gradual change would result in such widespread loss of confidence in medical knowledge that the condition of the public health would become much much worse before it could begin to improve. Faced with these difficulties, thoughtful physicians might try to find ways of introducing the new without altogether abandoning the old, or at least saving the appearance of the old as a vehicle for bringing in the new. The greatest burden would fall upon these new physicians, for just in trying to maintain the appearance of the old, the goal that they seek might continue to elude them. They would find themselves always on the boundary, no longer in the old and not yet in the new realm of medicine. They could not avoid the most terrible doubts about themselves as physicians and their vocation, about the new as well as about the old. It would be understandable if, at times, they gave in to the strong temptation to return to things as they once were, preferring the older practice for a professional life guided by abstract principle. Even if they struggled mightily to resist the temptation, its presence would be enough to confuse their thinking. We might imagine church theologians having the same kind of reflections about their calling. The conditions that make their work so difficult is the advance of secular culture. And, we might imagine that the theology of culture was conceived in just this way. The difficulty we are faced with in the case of theology is that we really do not know just what theology's goal is. We all know, or think we know, what health is, the health of the body or mental health, but the health of the soul, its ultimate well-being, is a goal that we can barely imagine. The theologian of culture believes that it is connected somehow to the unity of our cultural life, to the "meaning" of what we do and of what, essentially, we are. Suppose this is basically correct and suppose that this unity and this meaning and this essence are not as vague as I suspect they are. Even so, it may be that these goals will continue to elude the theologian as long as he tries to realize them as a theologian. And suppose this is so just because the theologian of culture still thinks of himself and his tasks in traditional ways, so that he cannot act in this new world of culture without imposing on its productions alien and unfriendly standards and he will not settle for a place in this world that is not a place apart; so that, whenever he tries to interpret or criticize the cultural life that is flourishing in freedom he misses the point, says what is irrelevant, yet he avoids embarrassment and maintains his dignity by speaking in a manner that conveys to some a sense of vague and enticing spirituality and profound thoughtfulness and, to others, confusion concealed by bombast.[92]

So, I come to my point. I believe that the theology of culture is self-defeating just because it is a theology and practiced by someone who thinks of himself as a theologian of culture, who enters the wide world of culture but, once there, directed by his religious principle, must establish for himself within it a place apart, a special pole or axis. But, the goal of the theologian of culture to protect and enhance autonomous life can be pursued constructively only if the he abandons any claim to a special role or a special standpoint and enters the wide world of culture in any one or more of its proper roles: critic, artist, philosopher, and so forth. Or, if being a theologian is what concerns him most, then he should openly identify himself with some tradition that he acknowledges to be his point of departure or his touchstone, but he should pursue his normative work always within the limits, self-imposed, of rational discourse and criticism. In fact, this is what Tillich appears more or less to have done. The availability of his writings to critical appraisal and the institutions of publication and teaching have guaranteed this. So, it is only necessary to make theory fit fact.

What kind of theory is called for here? First of all, it should be a theory about culture that does not deny religion or theology a place in the cultural scheme of things and that is not itself a theological theory. Such a theory would claim, first of all, that a theological standpoint is not a standpoint set apart but one among others and that religion is one sphere of culture among others. This describes the standpoint of the present and future protestant theologian, and this standpoint has at least prima facie justification. It represents the present religious and theological situation. Does this mean that the theologian may not attempt to construct a standpoint that envisions the whole of culture? Not at all. As the church theologian, who recognizes that religion is a part of culture, he may be properly solicitous of the welfare of society and want to bring to it the moral benefits of a religious life. Moreover, as Tillich observes at the very opening of his address, normative standpoints are not subject to a strict principle of bivalence, according to which the claim of validity for themselves entails the denial of it to others. However, Tillich doesn't explain this logical difference between experiential and cultural-scientific standpoints, and as we have seen, he soon abandons this joyous pluralism in pursuit of a more single-minded apologetic goal. So, let us inquire why normative-cultural standpoints have this freedom not granted to other scientific standpoints? First of all, I believe that it is because they are not theoretical standpoints, but rather they are the products of a certain kind of reflection. In the introduction to his third *Critique,* Kant distinguishes between determinative and reflective judgment.[93] Determinative judgments subsume what is given in experience under universal laws that are grounded in the categories of the understanding and the rules of their use. They are objective insofar as they represent no special point of view but the universal outlook of pure reason. Reflective judgments, on the other hand, are subjective. Although they, too, seek to subsume particulars under universal principles, the principles that they employ, while they may mimic the true universality of universal theoretical principles, are themselves derived

from and applied to the experience of life. My intention here is
not to follow a strict Kantian line but merely to borrow his concept of reflective judgment or, more simply, reflection. By means
of reflection, we make our way in the world, imagining what the
world must be like if it is to fit our experiences, our resolutions,
and our aspirations. It seems to me that this concept of reflection
fits nicely Tillich's theory of concept formation in the cultural
sciences, especially with regard to norms. At the same time, it
frees us from Tillich's tiresome preoccupation with systematic
construction and its embarrassing misrepresentations of cultural
phenomena. 'Normative systematics' is a misnomer. Rather normative thinking is reflective, occasional, subject to revision as fits
mood and circumstance. To be sure, the ideal of comprehending
all, of constructing a world, remains, but the process involved
here belongs to art rather than to science; it is inventive, does
not conceal its need to rely on illusion, and its ruling mood
is irony. Religious thinking, then, is a kind of reflection. Just
what kind of reflection ceases to be such an urgent problem. The
concept of religion is not a transcendental concept but a concept of reflection. It is likely that there are as many concepts
of religion as there are forms of religious life, and although some
of these may be virtually the same, there is no one concept that
fits all. That these cannot be reduced to a single concept of
religion is of no great moment. The academic study of religion
has flourished without a single standard definition of its subject.

If religion is just another kind of reflection, then the theologian cannot claim for its point of view any special transcendence even within the sphere of meanings. 'God' or 'the god
above god' or 'the one beyond being' are all meanings that play a
significant role within certain normative constructions of Western
religion. If they are said to stand for some special intuition, then
this reference to 'intuition' is just to another reflective judgment.
'Intuition' in this context expresses the value of a mood and need
not be and most likely is not cognitive.

The theologian, however, is concerned with more than the
construction of a normative vision. He wants to appraise such
visions or, at least, to appraise his own. He claims for himself the

right to distinguish between right and wrong versions of the normative visions that are associated historically with his own. Through this work, he develops capacities for more subtle appraisals, for in his search for criteria he enters the wide world of culture, and this digression may cause him to have further reflections about how the validity of his own religious vision may gain greater recognition. To the extent that his concern is only for the clarity and consistency of his reflections, he is a dogmatist; to the extent that his concern is to justify his vision to the world and, perhaps, to draw other worlds into his own, he is an apologist. In either case, the theologian stands more or less securely within the circle of his normative vision. But, according to Tillich, ethics is what drives the theologian out of the church.

Let us reconsider this exit. The theologian leaves the church to escape the intolerable condition of a consciousness divided between two competing, incompatible claims concerning normative ethics. However, as we have seen, the theologian of culture does not take refuge in the domain of secular-normative ethics but denies its possibility and establishes a theonomous domain within the wide world of culture from which he is the judge and indirect creator of all cultural norms. The impropriety of this move I have already observed, and I shall say no more of it. Instead, let us observe that 'normative ethics' can be interpreted in two senses. It can be interpreted, strictly or narrowly, as the system of rules or ends by which human actions are to be judged, approved, or condemned or, more broadly, it can mean the complete system of human goods or ends consistent with morality, that is, consistent with normative ethics more narrowly defined. If this observation is correct, the theologian will discover that normative ethics, defined narrowly, is not merely an escape route but a bridge. He will also discover the possibility of a theological-normative ethics in the broader sense. During his sojourn in the world, he will enjoy the freedom of reflection and he will find the moral criteria for deciding the validity of his reflective theological visions. Thus, he can move freely back and forth between church and world and pursue without conflict the dual goals that Tillich claimed for the theologian of culture. Although he may like to call his normative vision 'theonomy', he will now know that he has no right to claim for it any special privilege, that it is one standpoint among others whose validity is to be decided by the open discourse of rational appraisal. Theonomous visions will be subject to the same self-limitations of any autonomous activity. To find those limitations from within and not to impose them from without is an essential task of an autonomous culture and a right not to be compromised. The theologian will respect this right. In this way, the church theologian will avoid the conflicts outlined in Chapter 2.[94] He can be a creator without committing heteronomy. Moreover, he will no longer be committed to the obviously false claim that every cultural reality is religious, cultural, or otherwise. That there are and, therefore, that we possess the capacity to produce cultural realities that are perfect in their realizations, not only well formed but expressive, are facts that the theologian can acknowledge without qualification. This, however, does not close the door to the possibility of honest disputes over whether certain cultural realizations or ideals are religious. Beautiful art, which we may take to be self-sufficient and autonomous in its perfection may awaken longings that some may regard as religious and others not. It is also quite conceivable that a cultural ideal, envisioning a unitary culture, which expresses transcendental values, which embodies what many would take to be the noblest human aspirations, and which dares to praise these values in spite of the imperfection and impermanence that seems to pervade everything earthly would gain wide, perhaps, universal human acceptance and that human society or an appreciable part of it would realize a culture that exemplified this ideal. Even so, in spite of the unanimity, some might regard this ideal as religious and others not. In this free dispute, the theologian is free to participate. As to conflicts between religion and secular culture, the theologian will acknowledge that these have actually occurred and will not be bound by frivolous systematic constraints to deny their real possibility. But, he will also recognize that these conflicts would cease if all religious aspirations, and all secular ones as well, were kept consistent with moral rationality, with normative ethics in the narrow sense. Therefore, the theologian could share with secular

persons of good will an ideal of a society in which conflicts between religion and culture would not occur.

Yet the theologian may still be concerned about the truth of
his theonomous vision. Validity may not be enough for him. His
motivation concerning truth will not be like that of older theologians who believed that theological dogma is a saving truth
that must be believed. Rather, his concern will be motivated by a
noble desire that is consistent with morality but that secular morality cannot satisfy. Such are the great prophetic and apocalyptic
visions that express a righteous longing for universal justice, of a
justice that not only compensates but restores, that is able to
make right the enormous wrong that afflicts and deforms the
human past and present. Or, perhaps, the theologian is afflicted
with an extraordinary sensitivity to the suffering of others, especially innocents and children, by whatever cause, which sets
him on a quest for redress of cosmic injustice. Or, perhaps, mere
human praise of beautiful nature and moral nobility is not
enough for him and, in his heart and his mind, he longs for a
realm where these passing moments of beauty and goodness are
transfigured, made perfect, and never changing. Such visions are
characteristically although not exclusively religious or theological. But what makes them particularly fit for theological use
is that all of them carry human expectations beyond the ordinary
or the natural and beyond scientific justification. They involve
faith, and theologians are virtuosos of faith.

Once more, the goal of the theologian, the modern liberal
church theologian, is to promote human well-being, to enhance
life, to free human pursuits from every artificial and arbitrary
restraint except the self-imposed restraint of a rationally justified
morality. In behalf of this goal, he may forswear his concern
about truth. He may be convinced by Kant's refutation of the
theistic proofs, which, according to Tillich, have brought theology
down to earth, and he may be convicted by Nietzsche's charge
that transcendent longings are longings for death and not for life.
From Tillich, he may have learned to regard theological visions as
meanings, just that, which, although they may express the most
profound transcendence, are nonetheless purely self-referential.

This theologian will conceive of valid faith as a function of moral integrity and historical relevance. Agnostic with respect to truth, he also may suspect that beyond the world of human meanings there is no meaning that can become the basis of hope. For all he knows, human life on earth is a mere accidental episode, unlikely to be repeated, a moment in the natural history of a universe that originated from nowhere out of nothing and will eventually disappear, never to be recalled. This theologian will not be hoodwinked by Tillich's metaphysical pretensions that confuse meaning and reference. Perhaps, he will regard his theological task as transitional. His task is to guard against the dangers of reaction, fanaticism, and uncontrolled enthusiasm. In this role, his tasks and its problems are not unlike those of the new physician.

Nevertheless, the theologian's concern for truth may be too strong to allow him to remain content to carry out this restricted yet nonetheless valuable role. He knows that he cannot establish truth by the authority of his office. The truth that he is after must be the outcome of a free inquiry. Once again, the theologian must leave the church. But it may not be necessary for him to abandon his vocation as a theologian. For, after all, within the wide world of culture, there are theological traditions that are free, however esoteric and authoritative their origins may have been, and the theologian, in his inquiries may come to recognize that many of the elements of his reflective vision are derived from these traditions, so that he is free to reappropriate them, to fashion a new vision, a reflective vision that serves him as a directing faith, which does not guarantee the outcome of his inquiry but, at least, moves it toward some end. His aim, however, is not to perpetuate his old theological vision but to begin anew, not in Cartesian fashion by building certainty on an unshakable foundation, but, beginning where he is, he follows a course of free inquiry always open to self-correction and reversal. The theologian will find Tillich of little help in this undertaking, in this instance, not because Tillich denies that we have the capacity of free inquiry but because, on his interpretation of intellectual inquiry, the outcome of the inquiry is already decided. Free inquiry is a rite of passage, an initiation the theologian always undergoes within the framework of preestablished meanings. Theological modernism cannot be satisfied with such an archaic solution.

Nevertheless, the theologian is not without resources. There is, for example, Peirce's much neglected "Neglected Argument."[95] Peirce's argument makes itself especially available to us for several reasons, the most important of which is its starting point. No dogmatic assumptions, disguised or otherwise, are made. Its originating point is the pure play of the mind. Not self-interest but the disinterest and detachment of an aesthetical consciousness, "a certain agreeable occupation of mind," is its principal motivation. Moreover, it introduces us to a course of thinking that is as much scientific as it is religious and equally practical and theoretical. In its most common form, the argument is not a strict logical proof, it is not, to use Peirce's term, 'argumentation', but it is capable of greater and greater critical development and refinement, although almost everyone who employs it—and for Peirce this includes everyone—does not carry it beyond its initial naive reflective stage. In this respect, it is an argument whose various lines can be pursued by a community, by an open and culturally complex society, and, like all free activity that we pursue just for its own pleasure, it enhances life just because the outcome of the pursuit is not fixed and decided beforehand.

The theologian enters Peirce's argument by observing all that is around him. At this point, he is not yet a theologian nor a philosopher but an ordinary person who is sensitive to his surroundings and reflective. He is someone who delights in the power of sight for its own sake as well as in the pure activity of his mind, which, as it ranges over a variety of curiosities, finds within its own resources laws of increasing universality that fit them and explain their occurrence. He is a seer, a muser, who looks over the world back and forth and all around, who does not cease until he has taken in the whole, which means that he looks unceasingly. Nature, history, matters great and small, the spectacular panorama and the charming scene, all come within his view. He must also be a heart searcher, if his vision is to be complete. The rule that his mind obeys in his musings is freedom, nothing more. His passion is calm and self-disciplined, dispassionate, unromantic but not unfeeling, detached, with a good will, which is his only light, without envy and, therefore, capable of delighting in everything that he sees—except what is morally evil—honoring whatever is good, wherever he sees it. He does not survey the world with a desire to possess it but with a cultivated sensibility, knowing and discriminating, and not without sympathy. In this way, he envisions a world and fashions a rudimentary hypothesis concerning its divine origin, for in this way he fulfills his desire to praise the world and the abundant life that fills it. What better way to praise the world than to attribute its authorship to a maker supreme in intelligence and wisdom, that is, in skill and in the inventive power of choosing appropriate ends for his production, with a good will that is absolutely pure and with creative power that is without limit? Peirce's argument is an inductive argument, yet he seems to think that the outcome has the inevitability of a statistical certainty, of a conclusion that one cannot fail to reach, given sufficient time and freedom to observe and reflect. Unlike older arguments from design, however, that give the viewer little to do but observe and reflect on his own, Peirce's certainty is based upon the ongoing progress of human thought, which is the work not of an individual but of a human moral community. Perhaps the briefest way to depict the movement of Peirce's argument is to represent it as starting with Kant's third *Critique* moving in reverse order through the second to the first and back again to the third. It begins with the aesthetic, which it interprets in terms of the moral, and from a moral-aesthetic hypothesis, critical inquiry proceeds, for there is a morality of knowledge as well as of action,[96] and on the basis of all three, systems of knowledge are built. At this first stage the outcome of the procedure is prefigured: "in the Pure Play of Musement the idea of God's Reality will be sure sooner or later to be found an attractive fancy, which the Muser will develop in various ways. The more he ponders it, the more it will find response in every part of his mind, for its beauty, for its supplying an ideal of life, and for its thoroughly satisfactory explanation of his whole threefold environment."[97]

But, is this not just another theological vision? Does it not demean life by encouraging unwarranted flights of fancy? Nietzsche's proof that there is no god bears directly on this question.[98] Zarathustra introduces the proof in a moment of self-revelation. The scene is the Blessed Isles. It is a clear autumn day. Nearby fig trees are filled with fruit. The sea and the sky are pure and unbounded. "Once one said god when one looked upon distant seas," says Zarathustra, "but now I have taught you to say: overman." Which is to say, not god but man gives value and limitless potentiality to the earth and, therefore, is more properly thought to be its creator. God is a conjecture, a mere self-defeating thought of what is impossible and unthinkable. God, therefore, should not be taken as the exemplar for world creators, who rather must create only what they can see and think and feel. Then, in an intimate and confessional voice, Zarathustra introduces his proof: "But let me reveal my heart to you entirely my friends: *if* there were gods, how could I endure not to be a god! *Hence* there are no gods." The argument is valid, if the missing premise is supplied, namely that Zarathustra, who sees and thinks clearly and who has comprehended the world, does not desire to be a god, because such a desire is not for life but for death. A desire, if it is noble and life-enhancing, must be for something rational and perceptible. God is neither.

It would not be implausible, although it may seem too easy, to argue that Zarathustra's negative proof applies only to a conception of god advocated by a certain kind of mystic or speculative thinker, who prefers impenetrable mystery and irrational darkness to light, who when speaking of god uses images that cast deep shadows, that evoke terror and dread, instead of images like the clear blue expanse of the sky or the bright sun that make one glad. Thoughts of the negative sublime, which evoke dreadful moods, are not without fascination and pleasure for us and they do, on occasion, when properly thought, prove beneficial in shaping the moral life. But, if this be made a threshold to the divine, and if it be required before we are allowed to pass through it that we renounce life and its goodness and the self-confidence of thought and the beauty and sublimity of noble aspiration, we should rather renounce the divine and remain faithful to the earth. Thus far, Nietzsche is right, but perhaps he is wrong about the divine. Perhaps the key to divinity is just the ennobling vision

that the god contemplates. And if god is godlike just because he
revisions the world in the light of its most fulfilling archetype or
idea, something that in itself is intelligible even if it is not a
finished thought—ideas like truth, beauty, goodness, justice are
necessarily vague yet intelligible—then others who share this
vision and even in small ways create must know something of
what it is like to be a god and would not be blasphemous or
impious in wanting to be god or godlike. Such a thought could be
an expression of pure wonder and admiration. As to divine in-
comprehensibility, would it not be better to describe it as the
wonderful limitless magnitude of divine intelligence and wisdom
and power? These qualities come to mind repeatedly in our
musements and visions of the world and of the world's author
and also reflect the potency of visionary thinking itself, its lim-
itlessness as a resource for life, for growth and ever new possibilities. To call it divine is to give it the highest attribution of
value, one that, because of this attribution, is not made arbitrary
or capricious. If this argument has any cogency, then Nietzsche's
disproof may be set aside, and it may be assumed without contradiction that the aspiration to revision and refashion the world, to
be its creator, is a life-enhancing aspiration involving vision.

One might also argue, although perhaps not altogether seriously, that from the standpoint of Peirce, who, after all, is the
philosopher of Transcendentalism—Emerson, of course, is its
prophet—Nietzsche, who is no doubt an acute and profound
thinker, must appear afflicted with European pessimism. His humanistic vision ends in *amor fati* and the despair of eternal recurrence. Any would-be theologian committed to Nietzsche's doctrine of creation must cross the sea and enter into Emerson's
musings. For who is Nietzsche but Emerson's European echo?
Peirce did not think well of theologians.[99] He ascribed to them
the blame for the backward state of metaphysics, which by tradition they claimed for their domain. He depicts them as dog-
matists, who defend the faith by insinuating guilt into the con-
sciences of any who would deviate from the course or right
doctrine. They are corruptors of the morality of science, hypo-
chondriacs of the mind, their ruling motive is to conceal their

own unacknowledged religious doubt and cosmic pessimism. It is they who are the principal neglectors of the neglected argument, for they overlook or, in Tillich's case, deny the natural capacity of the mind to make sense of human existence in the world. In contrast to theologians, who are preoccupied with hidden gods and paradox and impenetrable mystery, doctrines that increase theological authority without clarifying thought, Peirce argues that if the reality of god be not a fiction,[100] a mere meaning, and if god be wholly good, then it is natural to expect "that there would be some Argument for His Reality that should be obvious to all minds, high and low alike" and "that this Argument should present its conclusion, not as a proposition of metaphysical theology, but in a form directly applicable to the conduct of life."[101] Tillich, of course, would recoil from this unqualified intellectual optimism. And yet, it is just this antipathy to optimism that reveals the profound inconsistency in Tillich's thinking: his inability to think of divine creativity except as a power that more often than not threatens and terrorizes its creation, and his conception of existence as an original self-positing act that is fatally self-disabling. So, in the end, it is to Peirce that I turn for help to rescue Tillich's idea of a theology of culture, of a way of thinking in the world that is free, creative, generous, whose highest motive is to transfigure all things in praise.

NOTES

1. Kant, *Critique of Pure Reason*, B595.

2. For more on this distinction see my "Tillich's Theory of Art and the Possibility of a Theology of Culture," in Jean Richard, ed., *Theologie et culture* (Paris and Quebec, 1988).

3. Plato, *Timaeus and Critias*, English translation by Desmond Lee (London, 1971), *Timaeus*, 92C.

4. Anselm, *Proslogion*, Chapter 2.

5. Gregory Vlastos, *Plato's Universe* (Seattle, 1975), 28.

6. *Timaeus*, 29A, 29D–E.

7. Friedrich Nietzsche, *Thus Spake Zarathustra*, Prologue, 3, English translation by Walter Kaufmann (New York, 1966), 13.

8. To modern thinkers, Kant and Hegel have ensured Plato's continued availability, the former by freeing transcendental ideas from transcendence, the latter by historicizing them.

9. Paul Tillich, *The System of the Sciences According to Objects and Methods*, English translation with an Introduction by Paul Wiebe, (Lewisburg, PA, 1981), 37. In this work, Tillich begins with thought itself and derives the different classes of the sciences from the operations of thought in its relation to being. In this system, the sciences of thought are given a pivotal role. The two basic logical laws that belong to the sciences of thought, the laws concerning contradiction and identity, prefigure the other two classes of sciences, the sciences of being, where thought encounters an other (is contradicted) and the sciences of spirit, where thought returns to itself.

10. Thought or spirit is still limited, not by the unfathomed world of beings that are other than thought, but by fate, by the exhaustion of creative power in a spiritual or cultural production. Cf. *The System of the Sciences*, 142–44.

11. Cf. *The System of the Sciences*, 67. Tillich distinguishes the sciences of being or empirical sciences from the sciences of thought in terms of their modes of cognition. Intuition is basic to the latter, perception to the former. "Perception becomes knowledge when reason establishes contexts. We call a rational perception 'experience,' and according to the basic attitude we also call the empirical sciences 'the sciences of experience' [*Erfahrungswissenschaften*]."

12. It should be noted that Tillich uses the term *Kulturwissenschaft* instead of *Geisteswissenschaft*. The former term was preferred by the neo-Kantians Windelband and Rickert because it seemed less metaphysically encumbered. Cf., Heinrich Rickert, *The Limits of Concept Formation in Natural Science*, translated and abridged by Guy Oakes (London, 1986), xii, 29, 64f. This should not have bothered Tillich. In *The System of the Sciences*, Tillich uses *Geisteswissenschaft*.

13. Wilhelm Dilthey, *Der Aufbau der geschlichtlichen Welt in den Geisteswissenschaften*, *Gesammele Schriften* 7:80, English translation by H. P. Rickman, *W. Dilthey, Selected Writings* (Cambridge, 1976), 170.

14. In a letter to friends written in 1917, Tillich includes Husserl's *Logische Untersuchungen* in a list of books he intends to study, and there are brief notes on it in a notebook that he may have kept then. However, the distinction between *Erfahrungswissenschaft* and *Wesenswissenschaften* or *eidetische Wissenschaften* is to be found not in that earlier work but in Husserl's *Ideen zu einer reinen Phaenomenologie und phaenomenologischen Philosophie*, first published in 1913. Cf. New edition, ed. by Walter Biemel, (The Hague, 1950), 21.

15. For more on the basic division of the sciences and the terms used to denote them, cf., *The System of the Sciences*, 65–66. Here, Tillich notes a similar division by neo-Kantians or epistemological idealists, who designate the division as one between natural and cultural sciences, and epistemological realists (Dilthey), who distinguish between natural and human sciences (*Geisteswissenschaften*). In the same section, Tillich expresses his distaste for the expression "natural science" as vague and misleading.

16. Cf., however, *The System of the Sciences*, 69.

17. This deficiency may be due merely to the limitations of space and time of a brief address. In *The System of the Sciences*, Tillich represents the physical sciences (physics, chemistry, geology) as *Gesetzwissenschaften*, sciences of law, whose aim is to subsume all of being under universal concepts or laws. These laws operate through time, sequences of entities obey them, but they are not historical, that is spiritual, but "rational and causal," that is, mechanical. The process of subsumption of being under universal laws is described by Tillich as a "titanic struggle." Cf. *The System of the Sciences*, English translation, 36, 57–59, 72.

18. On this last point, I have taken the liberty of reading into the text, what I judge, on the principle of hermeneutical circularity, implicitly to be there, namely, Kant's theory of the universality of aesthetic judgments of taste and his theory of genius. Cf. Immanuel Kant, *Critique of Judgment*, Part I, English translation by James Creed Meredith (Oxford, 1952), 136ff. and 168ff.

19. And, doubtless, also of its Aristotelian antecedents. A thorough source analysis of Tillich's concept of the concrete would take us back to Aristotle's concepts of *energeia* (activity, actuality) and *entelecheia* (completeness). Cf. Aristotle, *Metaphysics*, 1050a21. For the translation of these terms, I follow Montgomery Furth's translation: Furth, *Aristotle, Metaphysics, Books VII–X* (Indianapolis, 1985).

20. Hegel applies the expression 'objective spirit' only to the realms of law and ethics. Cf. *Encyclopedia*, part III, section II, English translation, *Hegel's Philosophy of Mind*, rev. ed. (Oxford, 1971), 241ff.

21. *Plan der Fortsetzung zum Aufbau der geschichtlichen Welt in den Geisteswissenschaften, Gesammelte Schriften*, vol. VII, 208 (my translation).

22. J. G. Fichte, *Science of Knowledge*, English translation by Peter Heath and John Lachs (New York, 1970), 99.

23. Why both the critical- and the normative-cultural sciences of art should not both be called philosophy of art may be unclear, at least it was to me until I recalled that Tillich's aim was to differentiate between the philosophy of religion and theology and to find for the latter a place within a system of the cultural sciences. Yet, this limitation of philosophy to the critical, theoretical phase of scientific work, divorced from content and concreteness and from normative insight, seems more due to apologetics than to scientific principle. This issue will be discussed more fully later in Chapters 3 and 4.

24. The same position is taken in *The System of the Sciences*, 44: Tillich claims that in the case of the sciences of thought and the human or cultural sciences, knowledge is directed not towards being—"which is essentially ungraspable . . . the abyss of knowledge"—but towards "thought itself, in the one case as pure form, in the other as norm. This is the problem of the ideal and normative formulation of concepts. It is directed towards existents that are not existents—a paradox for which logical terminology has introduced the concept 'validity'. . . . The concept 'validity' means that the form of thought stands over against everything real as both formation and demand."

25. Immanuel Kant, *Critique of Pure Reason*, B611–58.

26. Tillich's invocation of Nietzsche may cause some perplexity. Nietzsche's creator of visions, Zarathustra, is a free spirit, a solitary figure who comes forth from solitude only that he might share his vision, for which the world is not ready. He finds the world carried along by the illusions and false preaching of historical thinkers, schemers, functionaries, and this world, for him, is only a cause of temptation, the temptation to pity. He is not bound by the past nor by any chance circumstance, but of all historical things he is the redeemer, that is to say, he draws them up into his universal vision of the Overman as the purpose of earth. His only limitation is the circle of recurrence. Tillich draws back from the ideal of the solitary free spirit, warning that it leads to arbitrariness. Perhaps, in this, he was himself forewarned by Troeltsch against the dangers of an inward turning, historically indifferent spiritual attitude. Cf. Ernst Troeltsch, *The Social Teaching of the Christian Churches*, English translation by Olive Wyon, (London, 1931), 993ff.

27. Tillich doubtless would object to this characterization, because aesthetic judgments, as Kant conceived them, are reflective and are therefore without theoretical or

speculative cogency. Yet, this characterization is not inconsistent with what Tillich has said thus far. On the concept of judgment, cf. Kant, *Critique of Judgment*, Introduction, section IV, Meredith translation, I, 18.

28. David Hume, *A Treatise of Human Nature*, 2d ed. (Oxford, 1968), 17f.

29. If we consider this question retrospectively, from the viewpoint of the *Systematic Theology* (ST), a more definitive but no less ambiguous answer can be given. There, Tillich maintains a strict a priorism, but it is not altogether free from historical relativism. Thus, Tillich insists that ontological concepts, including the categories, are "a priori in the strict sense of the word"; that is, "They determine the nature of experience," they are "presupposed in every actual experience," but later he qualifies this as human experience so far as it is historical. Thus, he can say that 'a priori' does not mean "that the ontological concepts constitute a static and unchangeable structure which, once discovered will always be valid. The structure of experience may have changed in the past and may change in the future, but, while such a possibility cannot be excluded, there is no reason for using it as an argument against the a priori character of ontological concepts" (ST, I, 166f.). This view of the a priori is historicized Kantianism, or critical historicism. Earlier in the same work, in what reads like a eulogy of philosophical a priori concepts, Tillich contrasts the permanence of a priori concepts with the changing fortunes of philosophical systems, which come and go, "Only the general principles were left, always discussed, questioned, changed, but never destroyed, shining through the centuries, reinterpreted by every generation, inexhaustible, never antiquated or obsolete. These principles are the material of philosophy" (ST, I, 19). I think it fair to say that critical relativism or critical historicism is the position towards which Tillich is tending in this address. What remains of the older realism of ideas is the tone. Things are made permanent in human consciousness through praise.

30. Cf. Tillich's theological dissertation of 1912, where he interprets Kant's concept of "consciousness in general" as the idea of god as truth. He disputes Schlatter's characterization of this concept as an abstraction and continues: "This would be justified had the concept originated by abstracting from particular rational beings. However, it is rather the expression of the unconditional, supra-empirical, supra-individual validity of the acts of reason. Identity rests on this very foundation: that the particular empirical subject discovers in itself the necessity of reason by which it transcends all particularities." Paul Tillich, *Mysticism and Guilt-Consciousness in Schelling's Philosophical Development*, English translation by Victor Nuovo (Lewisburg, PA, 1974), 37f.

31. Kant, of course, was well aware of the danger that conceptual thinking might decay into mere formalism unless rules for their proper employment were laid down and carefully observed. Cf. *Critique of Pure Reason*, B193ff.

32. As in *The System of the Sciences*, pure being is said to be the absolute limit of thought; cf. 44.

33. I translate *Gehalt* as substance throughout the text because this is the term that Tillich uses as a synonym for it in the text, and as an English equivalent in such expressions as the "religious substance" of culture. (Cf., for example, *Systematic Theology*, III, 97.) The term *Gehalt* is untranslatable, not because of any inadequacy of the English language in contrast to German, but because, in German, it was made by Tillich to bear a meaning that it does not ordinarily convey. (There are antecedents for its use in Hegel, cf. *Encyclopaedie*, articles 558, 560–61, 563. Hegel, however, uses both *Gehalt* and *Inhalt* to denote the ontologically essential as opposed to the merely contingent content of an artwork.) Ordinarily, it means content. Tillich used it to signify an extraordinary content, a

metaphysical content of meaning that cannot be comprehended or rationally expressed, the ground or infinite power to mean something unconditionally. 'Substance', it seems to me, is an appropriate equivalent just because of its established metaphysical sense. I don't believe that 'import' conveys this sense, and although it has some currency in Tillichean circles, its use is more likely to hinder than to facilitate the understanding of Tillich. For discussion on the meaning of *Gehalt*, see James Luther Adams, *Paul Tillich's Philosophy of Culture, Science and Religion* (New York, 1965), and Robert Scharlemann, *Reflection and Doubt in the Thought of Paul Tillich* (New Haven, 1969), 36, fn. 15.

34. Cf., *Systematic Theology*, I, 6ff., 31f. Also his *Kirchliche Apologetik* (1913), reprinted in GW, XIII, 34–63; an English translation will appear in *Documents Illustrating the Development of Paul Tillich's Systematic Theology*, Victor Nuovo and Robert Scharlemann, editors, in preparation.

35. One should add, "and since Kant," for Kant's moral reinterpretation of Christian doctrine and of the church in his *Religion Within the Limits of Reason Alone* also has shaped modern protestant theology, and Schleiermacher's theological program depends upon it.

36. Cf. Friedrich Schleiermacher, *Brief Outline on the Study of Theology*, especially the Introduction, English translation by Terrence N. Tice (Richmond, 1966), 19–27.

37. This is a curious interpretation of the concept of autonomy. It seems more like a concept of copyright that Tillich has combined here with the belief that the correlation of standpoints is exclusive and unique. But, every science, even theology, is in the public domain—or it should be, for keeping it secret or esoteric is always a heteronomous action—and its user is obliged only to take proper care not to misrepresent it and generally not to use it to defeat autonomy. Moreover, while it may be proper from a particular normative standpoint to hold to a principle of uniqueness and exclusivity of correlates, there is no reason why this principle should apply across standpoints.

38. This, however, is not Tillich's final word on the historical church and its theology. He returns to it in the last section of his address.

39. Cf. *Philosophy in the Middle Ages*, edited by Arthur Hyman and James J. Walsh, (Indianapolis, 1977), 287, 450ff.

40. Representing, willing, and feeling is Dilthey's version of the basic triad of psychic functions. 'Representing' is a better term than 'knowing' for it takes in such noncognitive acts as interpreting and reflecting and wondering. Cf. Dilthey, *Ideen ueber eine beschreibende und zergliedernde Psychologie, Gesammelte Schriften*, V., 200ff.; and *Ausarbeitung der deskriptiven Psychologie, GS*, XVIII, 160f.

41. It is easy to confuse these different levels of psychic potency and actuality, to use terms that are supposed to denote one level to denote another. Tillich, on occasion uses 'function' where he means 'faculty', and although we can always make out his meaning, so that no harm is done, it is important to keep these levels distinct, for his argument depends upon it. We should, therefore, distinguish among (1) a psychic faculty or potency, which is the power and capability of the soul to act; (2) the activity itself that originates from this faculty; and (3) particular acts or instances of this activity, which may be taken individually or collectively. When taken collectively, we are dealing with a specific sphere of culture. (1) and (2) are abstractions and, as such, are always taken purely: the faculty of the will is not to be confused with the faculty of knowledge; willing and knowing are not the same. On the other hand, actual instances of willing or knowing or feeling always involve elements of the other psychic functions. For example, knowing that I lack the funds to pay my bills, may be accompanied by a certain feeling (a certain

quality of consciousness) and perhaps also by certain practical measures: willful self-deception, flight, etc. This is a rather crude account, it makes no fine distinctions within the faculties and activities themselves, but it is sufficient for the purpose of interpreting Tillich.

42. Tillich, nevertheless, remained loyal to this binary construction of the psychic faculties and functions. Cf., for example, *Systematic Theology*, I, 75.

43. Tillich now begins speaking of the religious potency as a religious principle. Does he mean by this term an arche or cause? It is not clear.

44. A variation on this view is Don Cupitt's notion of "hyperborean faith," which is religious but in a purely humanistic sense, and Cupitt's point of departure for this notion is Russell's "A Free Man's Worship," itself a candidate for a nonreligious interpretation of the No and the Yes. Cf. Don Cupitt, *The World to Come* (London, 1982).

45. The typology presented here is vaguely reminiscent of Heinrich Wolfflin's art historical typology of styles. Wolfflin's characterization of Renaissance art typifies the classic, whereas his characterization of the style of the baroque exemplifies what Tillich would regard as the religious type. Cf. Wolfflin's *Renaissance and Baroque*, English translation (Ithaca, 1966), 38f. and 58f.; and also Wolfflin's *Principles of Art History*, English translation (New York, n.d.). Tillich's typology includes a third type, on the far side of the classical midpoint, the predominance of autonomy includes varying degrees of the secular. It should also be noted here that the distinction between classical and baroque exemplifies the distinction between the aesthetic values of the beautiful and the sublime.

46. In *On the Boundary* (New York, 1966), Tillich tells of his constitutional antipathy to the classical: "Classical composure and harmony were not part of my heritage. This may explain why Goethe's classical traits were alien to me, and why the pre- and post-classical periods of Greek antiquity were more assimilable than the classical . . . the idea that the struggle between two opposing principles constitutes the content of history; the theory of dynamic truth, which holds that truth is found in the midst of struggle and destiny, and not, as Plato taught, in an unchanging 'beyond'," 15.

47. Cf. *Systematic Theology*, I, 79f., 112f., 172f.

48. From his several remarks about heteronomy, we might develop a system of historical types of heteronomy: there is an imperial or universal heteronomy that has been victorious over competitors in cultural formation; at the other extreme, there is an all but defeated heteronomy struggling to maintain its last defenses; and then there is heteronomy that seeks its own special religious sphere but at the cost of a divided human consciousness.

49. Tillich's concept of greatness underwent an evolution. While his concept consistently maintains its tragic and heroic aspect, its aristocratic and anti-bourgeois elitism, in his last and what must be taken as definitive treatment of it, he has drawn into it the rationalist-democratic concept of human dignity. Cf. *On the Boundary*, 19–24, and *Systematic Theology*, III, 88–94.

50. This is not a fanciful suggestion in the light of Tillich's charge elsewhere that modern culture is nominalistic and that the meanings it attaches to terms are manifold and ad hoc and, even when they attain a high degree of generality, lack the power of true universality. A critical or hermeneutical procedure based upon nominalist presuppositions therefore would miss the deep metaphysical meaning of terms that comes to light only when one attends to and participates in those revelatory experiences that disclose the depth of meaning. Cf. *Systematic Theology*, I, 44f., 122f., 177f., 255f., 260f.

51. "Whereof one cannot speak, thereof one must be silent." Ludwig Wittgenstein, *Tractatus Logico-Philosophicus*, English translation by C. K. Ogden (London, 1933), 188–89.

52. Cf., Arthur Danto, *The Transfiguration of the Commonplace* (Cambridge, MA, 1981), v–vi.

53. In what follows I have borrowed freely from Georg Simmel's essay, "The Constitutive Concepts of History" in *Essays on Interpretation in Social Science*, translated with an introduction by Guy Oakes (New York, 1980). My borrowing is free in two senses: I have helped myself to Simmel's examples and to his constructions, and I have adapted them to fit Tillich's theory of cultural science. Yet, the adaptation has changed them only slightly, for Simmel, who was a neo-Kantian and whose name appears twice in the text, was a presence in Tillich's thinking, perhaps an influence and perhaps, if we are guided only by the references in the text, a rival. For the particular examples I have selected, see pages 172ff.

54. Winston S. Churchill, *The Second World War*, vol. I, *The Gathering Storm* (New York, 1948), ix; vol. VI, *Triumph and Tragedy* (New York, 1953), ix.

55. Cf. *Systematic Theology*, I, 235ff. Cf. also Tillich's *Biblical Religion and the Search for Ultimate Reality* (Chicago, 1955).

56. *Timaeus*, 27–28.

57. Ibid. 53A.

58. *On the Boundary* (New York, 1966), 27–28.

59. English translation by James Gutmann, *Schelling: Of Human Freedom* (Chicago, 1936); for what follows, cf. 54–59.

60. I have not been able to trace this quotation from Simmel.

61. In his book, *Paul Tillich's Philosophy of Art* (Berlin and New York, 1984), especially the final chapter, and in Palmer's more recent unpublished paper, "The Place of Aesthetics in Tillich's Theology of Culture" (1986). I am grateful to Gert Hummel for making a copy of this paper available to me.

62. In *Der Blaue Reiter*, edited by Vasili Kandinsky and Franz Marc, English translation, *The Blaue Reiter Almanac*, edited by Klaus Lankheit (New York, 1974).

63. Cf. Franz Marc, "The 'Savages' of Germany" and "Two Paintings," also in *Der Blaue Reiter*, and Klee's retrospective lecture, *On Modern Art*, English translation (London, 1948) and my comments on the latter in my paper, "Tillich's Theory of Art and the Possibility of a Theology of Culture," in *Theologie et Culture*, edited by Jean Richard (Paris and Quebec, 1988).

64. *The Blaue Reiter Almanac*, 173.

65. Cf. Palmer, *Paul Tillich's Philosophy of Art*, 177f. As examples of Tillich's vague and rather unhelpful generalization when interpreting art, see Tillich's "Protestantism and Artistic Style," in *Theology of Culture* (New York, 1959), 68–75; and "Art and Ultimate Reality," *Cross Currents* 10, no. 1(1959):1–14.

66. Neo-Kantianism remains for Tillich the ideal or norm of philosophy, which is to say that it represents his experience of philosophy that has entered his own standpoint as the polar element opposite to the place of his own normative-constructive work. Even though Tillich was very much aware that there were other kinds of philosophy, he never departs from this normative and idealized sense of philosophy as a pure a priori science of concepts that defines the possibility of experience in general. Cf. *The System of the Sciences*, 158–75; also, *Systematic Theology*, I, 18–22. However, this should be contrasted with Tillich's "Philosophy and Theology," his inaugural address as professor of philosophical theology at Union Theological Seminary, first published in 1941 and reprinted in *The Protestant Era* (Chicago, 1948). Here the conception of philosophy as the inquiry into the meaning of being is Heideggerian. Heidegger's philosophy after the middle of the 1920s occupied another eminence on Tillich's intellectual horizon.

67. In *The Construction of the History of Religion in Schelling's Positive Philosophy*, Tillich's philosophical dissertation of 1910, he writes that "from the standpoint of the history of religion" post-Kantian German idealism must be regarded "as an expression of Christian religious life" and that idealism made this claim for itself. Cf. English translation by Victor Nuovo (Lewisburg, PA, 1974), 40.

68. The view that metaphysics is not a science but a religious expression is maintained and elaborated in the two major works of this period of Tillich's career: *The System of the Sciences* (1923) and *Philosophy of Religion* (1925), English translation in *What Is Religion?* (New York, 1969).

69. *The System of the Sciences*, English translation, 46.

70. Tillich's inability to free his thought from the bonds of older speculative motives may explain the relative lack of interest in his writings among hermeneutical and post-modern theologians.

71. Tillich quotes from the Prologue to the first part of *Thus Spoke Zarathustra*, English translation by Walter Kaufmann (London, 1978), 13f.

72. Ibid., 64. Read in its context, Zarathustra's utterance does not fit Tillich's interpretation of it. The nothingness implied in Zarathustra's utterance is not theological. It is the nothingness of self-doubt, which came upon him in his solitude. To give this a theological meaning is to beg the question.

73. Ibid., 228ff. The section referred to is entitled, "The Seven Seals (or: The Yes and Amen Song)." The preceding section, "The Other Dancing Song," should also be consulted, especially its coda, from which I quote the most pertinent lines. Zarathustra sings, "The world is deep / Deeper than day had been aware / Deep is its woe; / Joy— deeper yet than agony: / Woe implores: Go! / But all joy wants eternity— / Wants deep, wants deep eternity."

74. Ibid., 228. In this espousal of eternity also involved are the creator's higher aestheticism or sublimation and his love of fate.

75. Ibid., 93.

76. Tillich's interpretation of the categorical imperative, which Kant described as unconditioned in contrast to a hypothetical imperative, ignores this logical property of unconditionality or, better, replaces it with the sentiment of respect that Tillich then interprets metaphysically. Cf. *Morality and Beyond*, 74.

77. For a more sober and, to be sure, partly retrospective view of the social ferment of this period, cf. Tillich's *The Religious Situation* (first published, 1926), English translation (New York, 1932), 113ff. and especially 115: "The period of the revolution [in Germany after the first World War] particularly, with its eager anticipations, promoted an unrealistic enthusiasm which could not long endure. The actual power of the controlling capitalism and the superior strength of the bourgeois, rationalist temper which influenced all aspects of life were far too great to be set aside by a revolution, even by a successful one. Actual attempts to anticipate the realization of the socialist ideal in the organization of small communities, settlements, etc., failed unless they adjusted themselves to the general economic system. So the older generation of socialist leaders continues to hold fast to the bourgeois, rationalist elements in its tradition while young socialism remains without influence for the present."

78. Tillich gives no names, but one figure whose social doctrine must have figured prominently in this movement was Gustav Landauer, who, in 1907, wrote the following about social revolutionary movements: "In the fire, the ecstasy, the brotherliness of these militant movements, there rises up again and again the image and feeling of positive union through the binding quality, through love—which is power; and with-

out this passing and surpassing regeneration we cannot go on living and must perish." Quoted by Martin Buber in *Paths in Utopia* (New York, 1950), 51. Buber himself was an important figure in these movements.

79. For the contribution of neo-Kantianism to socialism, cf. Thomas E. Willey, *Back to Kant* (Detroit, 1978), Chapter 5, and also 174ff. for the connection between Eduard Bernstein's revisionism and neo-Kantianism.

80. The concept of love, as developed in Tillich's later writings, is complex. Indeed, it is not clear to me that it is a single concept; there are at least two. In one instance, love is a concrete norm of theonomous ethics (cf. *Morality and Beyond* [New York, 1963], 40), and as such, it is in correlation with a priori formal moral concepts. In another, it is the basic metaphysical principle or motivation in all of being, which drives all things towards reunion (cf. *Love, Power and Justice* [New York, 1954], 24ff.). If the first concept is meant here, then the mutual dependence of correlation is required. If the second is meant—and this is what the context seems to call for—then love does not depend upon form but, rather, form must depend upon love.

81. Kant's *Lectures on Ethics*, English translation (New York, 1963), provides numerous examples. A more systematic account is given in part II of Kant's *Metaphysical of Morals*, English translation in Immanuel Kant, *Ethical Philosophy* (Indianapolis, 1983).

82. *Thus Spake Zarathustra*, 48ff. Tillich misquotes Nietzsche here. He conflates the following lines: "It was creators who created peoples and hung a faith and a love over them: thus they served life. It is annihilators who set traps for the many and call them 'state': they hang a sword and a hundred appetites over them."

83. The distinction is fundamental to the advance of German idealism beyond Kant. For Fichte, intellectual intuition is the intuition of the original act of self-positing upon which all knowledge is founded. It is the ultimate autonomous act of reason. Cf. *Fichte: Science of Knowledge*, edited and translated by Peter Heath and John Lachs (New York, 1970), 45ff. For Schelling, as we have seen, the freedom that is intuited is not the freedom of reason but a darker freedom, demonic and dreadful. It is, in Tillich's terminology, the No, which of course for him becomes the Yes of grace. For a less complementary view of this mystical view of unconditioned reality, cf. Hegel, *Encyclopaedie*, articles 79–82 (English translation, *The Logic of Hegel*, translated by William Wallace, 2d ed. [London, 1892], 143–54). See also Tillich's earlier discussion of the distinction in his *Mysticism and Guilt-Consciousness in Schelling's Philosophical Development*, English translation, 73ff.

84. See note 48.

85. G. E. Lessing, *The Education of the Human Race*, esp. articles 72–78 in *Lessing's Theological Writings*, edited and translated by Henry Chadwick (London, 1957), 94–96.

86. The most fascinating and relentless application of this method of typological classification occurs in Tillich's *Systematic Theology*, I, 218–35, and III, 141–44. Here the substance pole is represented in its full religious dress as the holy that enters consciousness as a sense of ultimacy of unconditionedness or absolute power. The form pole is represented not as the pure form of autonomous thinking but as formed content, as concrete form, which human concern, even when it is overwhelmed by a sense of ultimacy, requires to fix its attention. The method as followed here is not one of mere classification. It is supposed to help us to understand the inevitability and the rightness that the course of history has taken. There is movement because the types at each pole are not fixed and pure but ambiguous and unstable. In every triadic construction, the third formation is not a classical synthesis of the first two (except perhaps when we reach the very end of the development), but a transitional state to a higher form of religious realization. In my

discussion of types of theology, I have made use of this construction as a guide for reasons that I hope will become clear.

87. In *On the Boundary*, Tillich writes of the effects of the 'Prussian ideology' on his own life and work: "These include the tremendous burden upon my conscience, which accompanies every personal decision and every violation of tradition, an indecisiveness in the face of the new and unexpected, and a desire for an all-embracing order that would reduce the risk of personal choice," 22.

88. As is well known, Tillich was active and a leader in the religious socialist movement in Germany during the Weimar period and fulfilled just this role. Cf. *On the Boundary*, 74–80; also, "Kairos," English translation in *The Protestant Era*, translated and edited by James Luther Adams (Chicago, 1948); "Religious Socialism" and "Basic Principles of Religious Socialism" in *Political Expectation*, edited by James Luther Adams (New York, 1971); and *The Socialist Decision*, English translation, edited and translated by Franklin Sherman (New York, 1977).

89. For the concept of self-defeating theories, I have benefitted from Derek Parfit's *Reasons and Persons* (Oxford, 1984), esp. Part I.

90. Cf., for example, *Systematic Theology*, I, 53ff.

91. The best version of Kant's ideal is presented in *Religion Within the Limits of Reason Alone*, Book 3, Division 1. For Rawls, see, *A Theory of Justice* (Cambridge, MA, 1971), Part 3.

92. Cf., Paul Edwards' well-known but rarely mentioned article, "Professor Tillich's Confusions," *Mind* 74, no. 294 (April 1965). Edwards' points are apt, but they lose some of their force for two reasons. First, his attempt to implicate other so-called metaphysical and Existentialist thinkers in Tillich's confusions is distracting and injects an element of vagueness into his claims. Second, he is uncharitable, and although charity does not guarantee insight, it does permit a critic to see beyond initial frustrations. At least in one instance, Edwards' exasperation with a particular text ("There are so many confusions here that it is difficult to know where to begin," 210) may have been the cause of his failure to read it carefully. Had he done so, he would have found that Tillich's confusion with respect to the meaning of negation is due to his failure to distinguish among logical concepts, transcendental categories, and the basic characteristics of existential awareness, a failure that is not common to other contemporary existentialist or metaphysical thinkers.

93. *Critique of Judgment*, Meredith translation (Oxford, 1928), I, 18ff.

94. See page 90.

95. C. F. Peirce, "A Neglected Argument for the Reality of God," in Charles Hartshorne and Paul Weiss, editors, *Collected Papers of Charles Sanders Peirce* (Cambridge, 1935), vol. VI, 311–38.

96. I owe this thought to my colleague Stanley Bates, whose lectures on Peirce first made available the rich resources of Peirce's thought for me.

97. Peirce, "A Neglected Argument," 318; on the "threefold environment," cf. 312. Briefly, they are pure ideas, "the Brute Actuality of things and facts," and the combination of these in the construction of a universe of meaning and scientific explanation.

98. *Thus Spake Zarathustra*, Part II, section 2, "On the Blessed Isles," Kaufmann translation, 86.

99. Peirce, "A Neglected Argument," 3.

100. Like Tillich, but for different reasons, Peirce believed it appropriate to attribute reality but not existence to god. Cf. ibid., 340f.

101. Ibid., 312.

Index

Victor Nuovo is Charles A. Dana Professor of Philosophy at Middlebury College in Vermont. He received his B.A. from Hope College, his B.D. from New Brunswick Theological Seminary, and his Ph.D. from Columbia University. His publications include the translations of Paul Tillich's two earliest books on the philosophy of F. W. J. Schelling.

The manuscript was edited by Gnomi Schrift Gouldin. The book was designed by Joanne Kinney. The typeface for the text and the display is Meridien. The book is printed on 55-lb. Glatfelter text paper and is bound in Joanna Mills' Arrestox over binder's boards.

Manufactured in the United States of America.

DATE DUE

APR 04 1991			

GAYLORD